Soular Reunion:

Journey to the Beloved

We are not complete without each other.
We are whole in each other complete.

DiadrAna
6/8/95

Soular Reunion:

Journey to the Beloved
A Manual of Love

By

John & Diadra Price

© 1996, 1997 Wings of Spirit Foundation

Published by
Wings of Spirit Foundation
6757 Arapaho, Suite 711, Box 345
Dallas, Texas 75248
(972) 233-2992

ISBN# 1-887884-05-X (pbk.): $12.95

10/97 Printed in USA
First Edition, 2nd Printing

Cover Art: *The Days of Creation: The Sixth Day*
by Burne-Jones, courtesy of the Fogg Art Museum
Harvard University Art Museums
bequest of Grenville L. Winthrop.

Wings of Spirit Foundation is a not-for-profit organization dedicated to the engagement of humankind in individual and collective prayer, surrendered to the Will of God [by whatever name], and to raising the consciousness of humanity to the realization of Oneness in Spirit. Through its endeavors, Wings of Spirit seeks to create an environment of harmony among all people and a world of peace.

Dedication

This manual is dedicated to the heart of every seeker on the journey to remembered union with Self.

Table of Contents

Introduction

This book is about the enfoldment and unfoldment, the involution and evolution, of God in manifestation. It is a grand journey, and we are not merely passengers along for the ride. Far from it!

We are today at a critical stage in the evolutionary cycle. We are crossing the threshold between the illusion of separation and the reality of oneness. We are awakening from our collective amnesia to re-member our Divine heritage and purpose as conscious co-creators. It is a time for reunion with Self and Source. It is the time for the ingathering of the sparks of Light back into the ecumenical Body or Communion of Light -- *fully awake.*

Reunion is the final stage in the re-awakening process. It embraces the totality of union possible in relationship to all creation. It begins with union with the inner divine Self, opening portals of consciousness to the awareness that we are far more than merely the sum total of our own limited thoughts and sensory experiences. It involves expanding our awareness to embrace the sum of all creation as One out of which all individuation emerged.

As we approach the portal of the millennium shift, we are awakening not only to the truth that the kingdom of heaven is within, but that it is much more expansive than we ever dreamed, *and* that we do not enter it alone. Once we are gifted with a glimpse of our individual oneness with and connection to God, the gift of that state in turn reveals that we are more than the sum total of our individual parts. We literally are connected with and woven into the soul fabric of *all* beings and *all* creation, just as we are eternally wed to the bride or bridegroom of our complimentary Self -- our Twin Soul.

The concept of the Twin Soul is an important missing link in this glorious involutionary/evolutionary journey, and it is an integral part of the process of reunion. It is a concept as ancient as recorded history. It embraces profound spiritual and mystical teachings, and it helps to explain the eternal yearning in the heart of man and woman to be united in oneness and love with one another. As you soon will learn, however, it is not just a romantic, make-believe myth. It is a powerful teaching which goes to the very core of Being. To fully understand the concept demands the vision of one who has experienced a certain degree of integration of Self, as well as the commitment to take full responsibility for soul action and life experience. Acceptance of the concept of the Twin Soul is not a prerequisite to benefiting from the teachings and principles contained in this book -- acceptance of Self is!

To you whose prayer has been to become the love of Christ, and who have said, "I want to be love no matter what I have to face within myself," this material is definitely for you. As you read, something within you will resonate with what you find. You already know everything that is printed here, you have simply forgotten. Be very conscious as the Knower within you kindles remembered union on many levels of yourself, and we encourage you to be ever mindful that as you begin to remember, your memory is quickening the same said memory of your beloved counterpart, your Twin Soul.

Also, be reminded as you read that every yearning of your heart is a prompted, seeded desire from the I Am presence of God within you to bless you with the fulfillment of that desire according to your chosen role in the Divine Plan. Your desire for more of God's goodness is a reactionary response to God's call for union. Your need to love and be loved is all part of the same said call. Your hunger and thirst for the companion of your soul is the gift that was given you in the beginning as you separated from a part of yourself in order to find yourself. Embrace your desire, your need, your hunger and your thirst as the invitation from on high beckons you to R.S.V.P. to the love that you are and to enjoy the fullness thereof.

We realize that this is a time of tribulation, confusion, chaos, fear and monumental change as the foundations of the past are crumbling to give way to a new beginning -- a New Genesis. As we pause in contemplation of our passage, we must not allow the shadows of our former selves to darken the path of Light beckoning us to the birth of our awakened Self.

Section One:

In

The Beginning

"In the beginning was the Word, and the Word was with God, and the Word was God. ... And the Word became flesh and dwelt among us, full of Grace and Truth: ... "

John 1:1,14

In The Beginning

"[K]now thou are one with the Cosmos,
A flame and a child of the Light."
Emerald Tablets of Thoth

I. Creation

"Light is the shadow of God."
Plato

"In the beginning, ... [t]he earth was without form and void, and darkness was upon the face of the deep ..." Gen. 1:1-2. All space was dark and devoid of matter. No spark of light or atom of matter existed throughout the infinite, timeless expanse. God is slumbering void. It was a state of perfect unity and uniformity -- an infinite sea of pure, primordial, incipient potential.

"And God said, 'Let there be *light*'; and there was light." Gen.1:3. From the darkness, *LIGHT* appears and consumes the void. The void awakens. This is not the limited visible light spectrum with which we are so familiar, but a superluminous, boundless, timeless, all-embracing, interconnecting energy-intelligence matrix which in-forms, en*light*ens, and enlivens all of creation. To the Chinese, this Light is "*chi*;" to the Japanese "*ki*;" to the Yogic traditions of India & Tibet, "*prana*;" to the Hindu, "*akasha*" *or* "*spanda*;" to the Taoists, "*Tao*" or "*Wu Chi*;" to the Polynesian, "*mana*;" to the Sufis, "*baraka*;" to the Jewish mystical Kabbalist, "*Ein*

Sof" or *"Endless Light;"* and to the Iroquois, *"orenda."* The Pythagoreans of Greece referred to it as the *"Music of the Spheres,"* and the ancient mystics called it the *"ether."* Modern quantum physicists might refer to it as the elusive *"grand unified force-field,"* the *"super-implicate order"* or the *"vacuum-based zero-point holofield"* (or *"Ψ field"*) In biblical terms, it is the *"Word"* or the *"Logos."* Some call it *"pure thought"* or *"superconsciousness."* To others, it is the *"One Form,"* *"primal vibration"* or *"animating Soul."*

   "[A]nd God separated the light from the darkness." Gen. 1:4. Metaphorically, from the numinous unitary state, God contemplated the vastness of itself, and infinite thought was thus contracted to a finite, but unbounded, point of reference -- what the Jewish mystics call *Tzimtzum* and modern physics refers to as a *singularity.* From the point of singularity, the formless, inchoate and homogeneous moved into differentiation and, ultimately, materialization. There is the birth or creation of contrast, duality, time, space and the material universe as we know it. As water churns into foam, so undifferentiated Source gives rise to the world. Light was thus made manifest.

   Modern physicists refer to this creation process as the "Big Bang," a moment *in time* -- in fact the birth of time -- approximately 15 to 20 billion years ago when all matter/energy in the universe was confined in an infinitely tiny pin-hole of space, from which it suddenly began expanding explosively in all directions at near the speed of light. Others theorize a much less explosive inflationary process of creation, more akin to a blossoming of a flower than a cosmic explosion equivalent to detonating one million, billion, billion, billion, billion one-megaton hydrogen bombs.

"God created the heavens and the earth." Gen. 1.1.
Light in its multitudes of form is the carrier and transmitter of
energy, as well as the generator of matter. As waves of radiant
energy expanded, a lowering of vibratory frequency occurred
and some were frozen into patterns at average speeds less than
the speed of light. Matter was created. Matter came into form
as condensed or trapped light, and it releases or emits light
when it decays. From this continuous cosmic dance, the entire
universe arose, from the smallest subatomic, partless particles
to the enormous stars and galaxies. Thus, the Light in-forms
the physical universe.

II. Involution

"Jesus said, 'If they say to you, Where did you
come from?', Say to them, 'We came from the
light, the place where the Light came into being
on its own accord and established itself and
became manifest through their image.' If they
say To you, 'Is it you?', say, "We are its
children, ..."
                              Gospel of Thomas 50

"[A]nd the Spirit of God was moving over the face of
the waters. ..." Gen. 1:2.   The Spirit of God *moved* within
creation. "Then God said, 'Let us make *man* in our image, after
our likeness ... So God created man in his own image, in the

image of God he created him ..." Gen. I:26-27. The image of God, the Infinite Light, was made *man*ifest in the world of form. The Spirit descended into creation in the form of the human Soul. As the Infinite Light is whole unto itself, it encompasses both polarities, male and female. The Hermetic Principle states, "as above, so below." As the expression of a Divine Idea in God Mind, humankind's Soul mirrored the image of God, likewise containing both male *and* female polarity.

"And God said ... "[b]e fruitful and multiply. ..." Gen. 1:28. The One became Two, and the Two became Many. The human Soul as the embodiment of the Spirit of God divided into greater and greater numbers, each containing a holographic image of the undivided whole from which it was birthed.

"God formed *man of dust* from the ground, and breathed into his nostrils the breath of life; and man became a living being.... God caused a deep sleep to fall upon the man, and while he slept took one of his ribs and closed up its place with flesh; and the rib which ... God had taken from the man he made into a woman and brought her to the man." Gen. 2:7, 21-22. In order to become active participants in the material world, it was necessary for the souls to be split into their masculine and feminine counterparts. Just as the Infinite Light of God had divided to create the material world, the human souls were divided to allow God-Man to consciously enter into that creation. The *Word* was thus made flesh. The "body" of God was incarnate through the immaculate conception of man/woman. And so, man/woman completed the involution of Divine Spirit into matter, albeit asleep to the memory of its divine and united heritage.

III. *Twin Soul Emergence*

"The Supreme state of human love is ...
the unity of one soul in two bodies."

Sri Aurobindo

Polarity is essential to all form. It was and is an integral part of the process of the involution or unfoldment of light into the world of matter. Positive and negative charges at the subatomic level of matter undergrid the entire physical world and are essential to manifestation. Every phenomenal thing is one of a pair of polarized opposites. For every positive charge in the universe, there is a negative charge to balance. It is this dynamic balancing counter-force which permits separation, fragmentation, time, space, motion and limitation. Polarity is such an integral part of the created world that physicists even posit the existence of antimatter -- for every particle, there is an antiparticle of equal and opposite charge. Without this electric symmetry, the universe as we know it would disappear.

Like the biblical story of *Adam* and *Eve*, virtually all of the ancient myths reference creation as involving the split of masculine and feminine polarities from an original state of unity. There is the Chinese story of *P'an-Ku*, describing the separation from their original state of unity of the yin (feminine) and yang (masculine) principles; the Egyptian *Atum* creation myth in which the air god *Shu* separates its two children, *Geb* and *Nut*, from their initial unitary love embrace; the Sumerian story of creation involving the uncoupling of the god *An* and the goddess *Ki* from their initially commingled state; the Akaddian story of the warrior *Marduk* splitting the body of the goddess *Tiamat*; and the New Zealand Maori story of the creation of the physical world by separation of *Rangi* and *Pappa* from their initial embrace. In the *Symposium*, Aristophanes references how the Greek god Zeus cut the souls of human kind in half, noting: "[m]an's original body having been thus cut in two, each half yearned for the half from which it had been severed.... [L]ove is simply the name for the desire and pursuit of the whole." And so Plato in the *Symposium* states: "The original human nature was not as they are now, but originally three in number; there was man, woman, and the union of the two."

The *Zohar*, "The Book of Radiance," is considered the most important literary work of the Mystical Jewish Kabbalah. It contains the following description of the descent of souls into the world:

> "When the soul is about to descend to this world, it first goes down to the terrestrial Garden of Eden. ... All initial souls [as exiting the treasury of souls] are compounded of male and female. When they go forth into the terrestrial world, the initial soul is divided into two separate entities, the two elements are separated. The intelligent life forces of the male function become clothed in a male corporeality and the female intelligent life force in a female corporeal body."
>
> *Zohar* III, p. 43

According to the *Zohar*, the spiritual structure of the treasury of souls is androgynous: it contains both of the masculine and feminine forces that produced it. It has an indeterminate gender, since it contains both genders in equal measure and balance. When the soul is ready to enter the body, however, it separates into its masculine and feminine components. Each half of the soul enters into a different body, one male and the other female. Birth represents a loss of original unity, yet the soul cannot accomplish its destiny except by moving into human form. As in Genesis, the *Zohar* states that at the hour of birth, the soul forgets all knowledge it has gained.

Patricia Joudry, co-author with Dr. Maurie Pressman of the book *Twin Souls: A Guide to Finding Your True Spiritual Partner*, poetically describes the entire process of the creation of the human soul, including the division of soul into its complementary masculine and feminine aspects, as follows:

> "In recurring cycles Father-Mother God pours itself forth into manifestation, later to return the perfected creation to itself. Through the interaction of its masculine and feminine principles, it begins the division of its one spirit into the many. In this first birth is established the pattern for the later divisions of the ovum-sperm into the many cells of the human embryo.
>
> ...
>
> In a continuous process of division, the divine energy descends into form. Throughout the universe groups emerge, each group harboring a multitude of souls-to-be. These are the 'cells' of the 'body' of God, and each is a life in itself.

The group souls separate into ever smaller units. As the groups separate, each of them is endowed with its own characteristics. The smaller the groups, the more closely the souls within them cohere. They memorize one another, even in the dim prebirth state. The longer the association, the more indelible will be the memory. ...

As the groups divide into their smallest configurations, there emerges a host of single soul-units. These are unformed souls. They are still only potential. Aeons must pass before they evolve to human state, yet they are whole in themselves, masculine and feminine together, containing all their unrealized potential.

Seemingly alone in the universe, filled with longing for the soul families from which they have been cut adrift, these entities must suffer yet another loss. There is a last, fateful division: each is struck in two, their masculine and feminine forces gathering into equal halves. Yet each retains the seed of the other, creating the polarity that will bring about the ultimate reunion."

Omraam Mikhael Aivanhov, writing in the 1960's in *Love and Sexuality*, part one, had the following to say regarding the nature of the Twin Soul:

"Every human being has a twin-soul. When man leapt like a spark from the bosom of his Creator he was two in one, and these two parts complemented each other perfectly, each was the other's twin. These two halves became separated, they took different directions, and they have evolved separately. If they come to recognize each other at any point during their evolution, it is because each carries the image of the other in the depth of his being, each has put his seal on the other. Thus, each one carries the image of this twin-soul within. The image may be blurred but it is there. For this reason, everyone who comes on earth has a vague hope that he will meet somewhere a soul who will be everything he needs, and that with this soul he will find indescribable harmony and perfect fusion.

Twin-souls complete each other; no other person in the world can so complete them. ... [T]wo souls whom God has created together are absolutely made one for the other, and nothing can separate them ..."

Through the refraction, division and mirroring of the Divine Infinite Light throughout the process of involution, a myriad of interrelated holographic images are created from complex interference patterns. When illuminated through consciousness, each point of light within each hologram contains and reflects the image of the Divine. Each soul represents a point of light, and each point of light reflects its divine polarity onto the canvas of life. And so, male and female -- the Twin Soul -- emerges.

Each of us has a Twin -- a complimentary counterpart, the other half of soul, the mirrored image and likeness of Self. Just as the soul contains within it the seed or image of Father/Mother God or the Infinite Light from which it came, each half of the split soul contains within it the seed or image of the unitary whole from which it was birthed.

IV. Evolution

"The consciousness of each of us is evolution looking at itself and reflecting upon itself."
Pierre Teilhard de Chardin

It is estimated that it took between 10 to 15 billion years for the earth to form out of the primordial sea of gases. The emergence of simple cell life on the earth took several billions of years. Several hundreds of millions of years ago, multicellular life arose. Tens of millions of years ago, mammals appeared for the first time. For 3.5 million years, humankind slowly evolved, from the first manlike beings called *Australopithecus*, into forms slightly less primitive, such as *Homo erectus*. It was not until approximately 350,000 years ago that the earliest forms of *Homo sapiens* first appeared, with the modern *Homo sapiens* not entering the picture until slightly over 100,000 years ago. Only 70,000 years ago, Neanderthal man first appeared. Interestingly, Neanderthal man can be traced to be a further natural evolution of *Homo erectus*. The closest ancestor to the modern human, *Homo sapiens*, however, appears to have no direct connecting link with the earlier primitive forms.

Since the time that humans first dominated the scene on earth, physical evolution has nearly come to a halt, except for minor variations. No major new species have emerged during the last few million years. That is not, however, to say that there have not been major evolutionary events since the advent of the human being. It is estimated that "thinking human" first emerged approximately 50,000 years ago. From that point, language appeared. Humans became reasonably self-analytical, and the first civilizations are typically dated to have arisen starting about 5,000 years ago. From then, the pace of advance has quickened. Within the last 500 years, we have gone through the Renaissance and the industrial revolution. Within this century alone, humankind has split the atom, harnessed nuclear energy, commenced outer space exploration, invented the computer, and brought itself to the point of virtual instantaneous communication worldwide. Simultaneously, humankind has entered into the Atomic Age, the Space Age, the Information Age and the Computer Age. In the span of a tiny fraction of the history of the earth, humankind has literally moved from the cave to the cosmos. In the words of the U.S. Astronomer, Carl Sagan:

> "Image the fifteen-billion-year lifetime of the universe compressed into the span of a single year. Dinosaurs emerge on Christmas Eve; flowers arise on December 28th; and men and women originate at 10:30 p.m. on New

Year's Eve. All of recorded history occupies
the last ten seconds of December 31 ..."

And what a 10 seconds it has been. The ancestors of the
modern human could never have begun to envision the
possibility of advancements now deemed commonplace.

"[H]uman imagination in the past was never
great enough to imagine the kind of future that
actually became the present."
C.F. von Weizacker

It is hard to imagine what the next 5 seconds will be like.
Global information continues to double in shorter and shorter
periods of time. It doubled from the time of Sumeria to 1900
(6,000 years); again from 1900 to 1950 (50 years); again from
1950 to 1970 (20 years); and again from 1970 to 1980 (10
years). It has been estimated that by the first 6 months of 2012,
global information could double each day. During the 2nd 6
months of that year, it could double each hour. By 2013,
doubling could well occur each and every second. At this pace,
all manner of record keeping, data storage and retrieval would
be rendered obsolete.

Something happened in the time-frame between 5,000
to 50,000 years ago -- an epigenetic turning point. Humans
became self-reflective or self-conscious. Just as God
contemplated itself (Divine Mind contemplating or turning
inward on itself), humankind pondered itself. Suddenly,
evolution was no longer unconscious, passive, receptive and
automatic. Human beings became *agents* of evolution.
Involution and the process of physical evolution were essentially

complete.   Spirit was now joined with matter, and the awakening of Spirit/matter had begun.   It was the commencement of the evolution of consciousness, the beginning of the process of awakening, the first step in the journey of re-membering.

There is much conjecture as to when the soul of man/woman first appeared in human form on the earth. Some believe that the united souls were the gods referenced in myth who actively participated in the creation of all of the worlds in the universe (or multiple dimensions of universes) and the many life forms inhabitating those worlds, including the earth. According to these, the souls may not have descended into human form until the process of physical evolution was nearly complete. Others opine that the souls descended into form early on and, along with all other physical evolution, slowly evolved into the human form as we now know it.

Perhaps, we are not yet capable of fully understanding creation and/or our exact role in the physical evolutionary process. One thing, however, is clear: humans have played an essential role in the process of advancing along the evolutionary spiral to this point, and humanity now stands at another pivotal turning point. Just as our Twin Soul nature was and is essential to bringing us to this point in evolution, it also will be the catalyst (encoded within the fiber of our being) which will impulse us into our next evolutionary stage.

V. Reunion

> "Reunion is reidentification with The Source We
> Are...We do not 'arrive,' we process. We do not
> 'learn,'we remember. We do not 'become,'we are."
> P.M.H. Atwater, *Future Memory*

As you will see as you progress through this manual, the importance of this subject at this time is not to encourage or assist individuals in searching for or locating their Twin. While we believe that Twin Souls are now being brought into direct conscious communication, spiritually and bodily, more frequently than ever before, this is due to the advancement in evolution of the consciousness of individual soul. The reunion of Twins is the result of the awakening of more and more souls to their own divine nature, as we begin the process of re-membering who we truly are. It is an inevitable consequence of the next step in the evolution or ascension of consciousness.

Teilhard de Chardin says that "to complete ourselves, we must pass into a greater than ourselves." It is not man or woman alone who represents the image of God. Rather, the image is only actualized through their relationship. It is through the complementarity of man and woman that the image of God is developed and deepened, and it is only through relationship that we participate in the image of becoming God. In Teilhard's words:

"It is not in isolation but in paired units that the
two portions, masculine and feminine, of nature
are to rise up toward God. The view has been
put forward that there can be no sexes in Spirit.
This arises from not having understood that
their duality was to be found again in the
composition of divinized being."

Teilhard refers to the "New Genesis." It is a time when the
energies of love and union must be mobilized and harnessed in
order to take us to the summit of the convergence of the forces
of evolution. In order to burst through the next peduncle and
reach "Omega Point" requires an "act of love." It involves
"moving to a centre-to-centre relationship" with Self, with
others, and with God. Relationships provide the mirrors which
light the pathway of ascension. They lead us to the balanced
stillness of unity from which we sprang and to which we are
destined to return.

The most intimate relationship, of course, is that of self
with the Twin of its Soul. Through the complementarity of the
pair, each draws the other along the path of ascension. As we
are able to open ourselves to the guidance of our own inner
divine nature, we move closer and closer to that centre position.
We get in touch with Self, we reach an inner state of equilibrium
and harmony, and conscious communication with the Twin is a
natural consequence. In unison with our Twin, our
consciousness expands, an awakening occurs, and we begin to
re-member our divinity. Ultimately, we are reunited with the
other half of Self, and we assume our destined roles as
conscious co-creators.

The *Zohar* refers to "Man," the result of the union of masculine and feminine in God, as having been created as a vehicle for God's own self-fulfillment. The cultivation of the spiritual powers in humankind, and the union of masculine and feminine souls on earth, is viewed as indispensable to God. According to the *Zohar*, humankind was created as the agent for the reunification of God. Reunion of the masculine and feminine (of the Twin Soul) is part of the process of the ascension of the soul, and it leads to immortality.

Twin Soul reunion does not represent the end to the story of creation. It is the beginning of a new age, a new consciousness, a new birth, a new creature, a "New Genesis."

> "Man's whole reason for being is to gradually pass through his millions of years of physical sensing into his ultimate goal of spiritual knowing. Man has now reached a transition point in his unfolding where he must have that knowing. He can acquire that knowing only through greater awareness of the Light of the universal Self which centers him as One with God."
>
> *Walter Russell, The Secret of Light*

Like it or not, you are on a collision course with your spiritual destiny with which you shall soon come face to face. It is inevitable. Are you prepared to stand naked before the mirror of your Self? Are you ready to pass through the initiation of fire? Are you ready for Twin Soul reunion?

Section Two:

The

Call to Union

"We are the joint will of the Sonship, whose wholeness is for all. We begin the journey back by setting out together, and gather in our brothers as we continue together."

A Course in Miracles

The Call to Union

Every heart is beginning to sense the call from Spirit to enter into a greater experience of union with the Divine. It is felt as a yearning to know Self at a level of intimacy which far surpasses present awareness. It is felt as a desire to go home, to find something which seems to be lost, to fill a large, hollow, empty space within self. It is felt as the need for fulfillment in relationships, the desire for intimacy with other. For some it is felt as the desire to find a soulmate or your Twin Soul. Some feel it as just the opposite, the need to be alone and apart from the maddening crowd, the need to get away to the mountains or the shore by themselves. Others feel it as a yearning to serve humanity, to find their mission, their people, their right and perfect place.

The calling you feel in your heart has brought you this book wherein hopefully you will find a greater understanding of this call and validation for the experiences that are now being placed before you. Never before in the history of humanity has this call been felt by so many. Never before has the consciousness of humanity been as ready for the degree of union that is about to take place.

It is this new degree of union that will be addressed in these pages. It is what you have been seeking all your eternal life. It is what you desire above all else because it is your unremembered destiny that is written in your heart, and the time has come for that which is coded to become your intimate experience. We are far into the return journey to paradise lost. We have long since passed the halfway mark, and we now stand before the portal of the kingdom within in proportions of critical mass where a few mystics of old stood before us.

We are speaking about remembered union with the Divine as the experience of oneness outside the reference of time and space. We are speaking about the experience of eternal life in which there is no sense of separation, no awareness of lack or not enough. It is the experience of having all and owning nothing, of feeling full and empty at the same time. It is a state of being whole and complete within Self while, at the same time, recognizing the greater completion of Self within our collective oneness in this dimension and beyond. It is the experience of timeless time where past, present and future converge in I Am. It is the experience of the Word made flesh -- as above, so below.

It is a time of great change as this shift of awareness begins to take place collectively. Change, not only for those who are *consciously* on the path of spiritual evolution, but change for all. Everywhere you look things, people and situations are shifting, moving, transforming, healing and being released. It is a time of closures, new beginnings, discoveries, mysteries unveiled, pasts revealed and prophesies come to pass. We cannot escape our destiny of remembered union with the Divine, and *all* is Divine.

It stands to reason, as we approach the final days of consciousness lingering in the residue of the sense of separation, that all that remains of the veils of this illusion will accelerate in rending free. That explains why you are now fully immersed in the *end times, the last days, the final judgments, the fears come to pass, etc., etc.* This great truth will help you understand why some of you are presented with the opportunity to experience the laws governing consciousness in accelerated proportions. This is why every false identity of self is being wrenched from your possession; all paradoxes are being asked to be reconciled, all differences allowed, and all opposites embraced. This should explain to you why you are being asked to give up everything and accept everything, and why things, people and situations are falling away or leaving your proximity which are no longer for your highest good or which delay your experience of union.

Many of you are obsessed by an urgency to purify the soul of painful memories which continue to create undesirable feelings and emotions dictating out of control behavior patterns. All of you are being shown where self identity is still hanging on to titles, positions, roles, status symbols, and monetary values. You are being drawn into relationships and situations that require karmic cleanup, and you are being removed from social status symbols. In all this, it is the best of times and the worst of times for each of you depending on the degree of your resistance to that which is required for release and acceptance.

As we enter this *Golden Age* of the call to reunion, we will become more and more aware that the final process of all this will lead us more and more into the importance of *relationships,* for only in relationships will we be able to fully recognize the degree of attachments and misnomers of consciousness that need to be exchanged for the word of truth. Only in relationships can we truly measure our progress of the states of consciousness we think we have come to realize through prayer, meditation and self analysis. We must have an object which serves as a point of reference and an opportunity for resistance in order to truly know if we have become the nonjudgmental, unconditionally loving, unattached, possession-less individual we know we must become in order to experience the remembered union with the divine Self which exists within us as these perfect states of awareness. It is only when we are in relationship to something or someone that we can evaluate our ability to *be* the livingness of the true nature of who we are. Only when we can *be I AM* fully remembered in relationship to all will we come to know and experience union.

You will be asked to be in relationship with the silence, your thoughts, feelings and emotions, your jobs and careers, your children, family and personal possessions. You will be asked to be in relationship to your pride and prejudices, judgments, sense of guilt, honor system, evaluations, priorities, hidden agendas, belief system, all ego fear states, the full spectrum of self, and, finally, you will be asked to be in relationship with a significant other, soulmate, or your Twin Soul.

Again, we reemphasize, you will not know the fully realized state of awareness within you until you are in relationship with something or someone who mirrors back to you your current state of mastery.

We are becoming fully conscious creative beings, aware of our divinity and our unity, aware of our collective as well as individual specialization as an integral part of a divine plan in creation. In the beginning, we were all one in the one and only God I AM, but we were not aware of our oneness in ourselves or our collective. And the great God said, "let there be...", and we became the image and likeness of God, complete, whole, male and female in one I AM image sent forth to become fully conscious, fully co-creative, and, finally, fully creative as a realized being of the I Am that I Am. We were sent out on a journey, a journey of awakening and remembering, a journey of discovery of the Divine within. It has been a very long journey of involution and evolution.

In our masculine or feminine expression of the one I Am Self that we are, we have been given the opportunity to experience the totality of that masculine or feminine energy. We have experienced every possibility for creation in a polarized universe. We have experienced all extremes and measures. We have discovered self and Self and all the universal principles of Truth that govern our existence and our experience. It has been an individual journey of awakening our male or female nature to all possibilities of Self creation. We have labeled some of the journey good and some of the journey bad. We are being asked now to reconsider these judgments and recognize the totality of the journey as neither good nor bad, but simply a journey of learning and awakening to all possibilities in co-creatorship.

Whether you are single, married or in an intimate relationship, we hope you will realize the depth and true meaning of our proposed idea of the importance of awakening to the concept of spiritual transformation through relationships.

Those of you living alone are being given the greatest opportunity to be in relationship to yourself. You are experiencing the relationship to being and living alone. You are immersed in your relationship to your own space, thoughts, dreams, preferences, choices and independence. Being on your own has provided the opportunity for extended prayer, reading, listening and focus, for trust at incredible levels and for stewardship of self responsibility. It is a glorious time for Self discovery.

Some of you are living with a spouse or significant other, yet you find it much like what you would imagine it to be like living alone. You and your partner seem to be living separate lives but sharing one roof. You go your way and they go theirs. In giving your partner their freedom to do and be, it has given you the same opportunity. You have found time to study, pray, read and attend functions of interest to you. You, too, have come to know yourself at a deeper level.

Then there are those of you who are very much involved in intimate, active relationships in which you either get along or don't get along or both. The point is, you are actively involved with each other on a constant basis. This, too, is the perfect opportunity being given you to come to know yourself, for you know by now that active relationships mirror all aspects of *you*.

We wish to make one thing very clear about the material you are about to study. It is all about the awakening, discovering and reunion with Self, and Self in every aspect of Self. It begins with individual Self discovery. Then and only then will you be drawn into relationships which are expanded extensions of your Self.

Many of you who have picked up this book are looking for the companionship and fulfillment that a soulmate or Twin Soul will provide. Granted, there is glorious intimacy and fulfillment to be experienced in these relationships, but you will not be drawn into the proximity of that type of relationship until *your* realization of Self reaches a vibrational frequency of Self love that attracts that same said frequency of Self love in another. We cannot work outside the laws of consciousness.

The laws of consciousness assure us of attraction equal to our conscious vibration.

Unconditional love is the energy of awareness that begins the magnetic attraction of union with Self and other aspects of Self. You have been on a journey of unconditional Self love discovery all along, and to the degree that you have found that within yourself will you attract your counterpart or complimentary opposite gender of Self to you. Remember, reunion occurs through the magnetic attraction of unconditional love vibrations which are equal to the divine essence of the unconditional love vibrations at the center of that which has been created. Like attracts like.

Now, for those of you looking for your soulmate or Twin Soul, forget it! You will not find this person until you find yourself. Because of the law of attraction, you will always draw into your life a relationship that is equal to the state of consciousness being expressed by your awareness or belief system. We all want the perfect Prince Charming or Cinderella who completely understands us, loves us unconditionally in all of our forbidden states, allows us unlimited freedom, and thinks exactly like we do. Only to the degree that you can *be* that person you desire to attract will they show up in your life.

For this reason, we have put great emphasis on the Seven Sacred Mirrors of Relationships. This section will help you awaken to the depth of unconditional love that is being expressed by you in any given moment. It will help you see the state of consciousness that is being mirrored back to you in every kind of relationship, whether it be a situation, a feeling, a thought or a person.

You will be taking new eyes into every relationship after studying this material. Much will be revealed to you! Some of the revelations you receive about yourself will make you want to weep. Others will make you want to shout for joy, but all revelations will awaken from your own heart which already knows these truths.

Those of you who are beginning to feel or who have felt, from the time of your arrival on earth, the yearning to be united with another, know this is a cosmic, coded, divine calling which is awakening in you the experience of the reunion you desire. There is another aspect of yourself out there somewhere in this world or another that is the masculine or feminine counterpart of the complete and whole you seeking reunion with itself. All the relationships you encounter along the way are gifts of God I Am in others to help you become the master of unconditional love, so that you can attract that whole and complete other Self into conscious reunion.

Many of your encounters are accelerated karmic opportunities for resolution, and prime opportunities of rapid advancement. Do not avoid them if you wish to meet your soulmate or Twin Soul. You must take care of them first!

A soulmate is someone whose resonating energy field is very close to your own in the process of awakening to true Self. You may have many soulmates along the way who are beings of Light who share a mission and purpose with you. They will be attracted to you more and more as you expand your unconditional love vibration, but do not fall into the erroneous belief that soulmate relationships are all love and glory. They will reflect to you many pastures within yourself that need to be explored. A soulmate is one who may just love you enough to show you all the aspects of self that need to be brought into the light of unconditional love. The very one you have the most difficulty accepting may be a soulmate who is giving you the opportunity to forgive seventy times seven. They will often create an environment of safety for you to empower you to process your *end times*. They will teach you the depths of unconditional love in preparation for the reunion with your Twin Soul. Soulmate relationships are certainly the gift of God's grace in the process of reunion. We encourage you to seek unconditional love within Self first, and then be completely open to a soulmate relationship that will bless you and accelerate the path of reunion for you both.

Twin Soul relationships are another entity all together, for a Twin Soul is the other half of you, the exact you in your complimentary, polarized opposite Self.   As your complimentary Self, reunion with your Twin is truly heaven on earth.   There is no other love like it.   Your vibrational frequencies are exactly alike.   Your soul is identical.   Your dreams, mission, and purpose for being are the same. First encounter with a Twin Soul is pure bliss, ecstasy, the knowing of oneness.

Meeting your polarized opposite Self, however, can create an opportunity for unexpected tribulation. That will be determined by the degree of total acceptance you have acquired for everything that is of the opposite polarity of your masculine or feminine Self. Because you are a perfect mirror of reflection for one another, nothing remains hidden. You stand before yourself naked and fully exposed. Have you awakened to pure unconditional love? Are there no hidden agendas? Have you become fully Self realized?   Are there no more active programed behavior patterns left that protect the alter-ego? Is there nothing more to forgive? Has all sense of separation been dissolved? If so, your reunion will be the most awesome experience of your life, and you and your Twin will set out to accomplish a mighty work of service. If there are still illusions of consciousness occupying soul space, however, you will be required to face these illusions together and walk through the fire of final soul purification. This is often referred to by Twins as entering the battle of Armageddon. If your Self love is strong enough, however, the battle will be won by the Oversoul of the indwelling Spirit that is shared by you both, and you will conquer. Once the battle is behind you, you will walk together forever in the eternal life consciousness of oneness. New dimensional realities will be opened within you, new assignments will be given, and the glory of God will reign forever in those whom God has joined together.

Beloved, the one you are looking for is the one who is looking. Find this one, and the one whom you think you are seeking will find you.

Enter now into the study of the Seven Sacred Mirrors of Relationships. They will reveal to you the depth of the cosmic eternal laws of creation, and the magnitude of the glorified being of love and light that you are. They will provide tools for transformational understanding, and guide you into the depth of your soul. They will lead you down the straight and narrow path of unconditional love and finally into the arms of your Beloved.

Section Three:

The Seven
Sacred Mirrors
of
Relationships

"We will be stripped naked and utterly open, so that we can become the mirror in which the face of infinite beauty is reflected -- the mirror in which our beloved Twin can gaze and see the perfect Light he or she is."

DiadrAna

The glory of our Lord
stands before each mirrored Self
to
reflect its own image.

Look with the eyes
of the heart.
See your own idea.
Clothe it not.

DiadrAna 12/12/95

The Mirrors of Self

Love and Wisdom expand consciousness directly proportional to our ability to *live* the truth that we have gleaned with the mind. As we seek to become more fully re-membered in our capacity to love and be loved, we will find that relationships are the barometers by which we measure our degree of expansion. Without experience in relationships we have no point of reference in knowing exactly who we are and where we stand in our spiritual evolution. How will we ever know if we have mastered false judgement unless we are faced with a situation or individual upon which to focus our attention? How will we know if we can love unconditionally unless we have the opportunity to apply the love vibration to a situation or person that is in close proximity? How will we know we have conquered fear unless we are willing to face that fear and see it for what it is?

Not to worry! Consciousness is a magnetic field of attraction in alignment with immutable spiritual laws, and we are beings of consciousness. As our Spirit continues to expand the knowledge of wisdom and love within us, we will attract relationships that will reflect the depth of that wisdom and love as it integrates with present awareness. Every relationship and every situation becomes a mirrored reflection of deeper and deeper levels of consciousness until, face to face, we stand before ourselves unveiled.

We believe our spiritual growth takes quantum leaps in the presence of relationship. Relationships are always two or more gathered in the name of Love. Whether Love is recognized or not will be determined by the eyes beholding that which they beholding. Willingness to enter into all relationships with the intention of unconditional love in the heart and the "single eye" of the mind will guarantee a vision of oneness and integration that will lead the soul into the path of ascension to God.

The Seven Sacred Mirrors of Relationships* addressed in the following pages are, in essence, one mirror reflecting deeper and deeper pools of inner vision into Self. Clear insight into one opens the door to the next. They are as progressive in nature as the stairway to heaven and the "open Sesame" to the kingdom within. No person and no situation outside of you is in your life for any other reason than the attraction of the vibration of your magnetic field, thereby mirroring yourself. They stand before you with their gift in hand -- an opportunity to see and experience a greater capacity to love and be loved. Ultimately, they hold for you your freedom, though sometimes they appear to offer you bondage. Look deeply now into the heart of the ONE who stands before you. Find yourself and, when you do, your vibrational magnetic field of attraction will draw your counterpart of identical resonance to you.

---

* We wish to acknowledge our adaptation and incorporation, in part, of certain concepts eloquently expressed by Gregg Braden in his intensive seminar materials and new book entitled: *Walking Between the Worlds, The Science of Compassion*, Radio Bookstore Press © 1997.

Mirror Number One:

The Mirror of Your Vibration

(Your magnetic field of attraction: like attracts like and opposites attract)

This is the mirror of your present state of consciousness that reflects directly back to you, in exact measure, what you are outwardly expressing and doing as the result of your own inner posture. Your actions are in direct alignment with your feelings, emotions, beliefs, judgments, etc., and your current reality is directly proportional to those inner vibrations. Relationships that are drawn to you for viewing this mirror of self will show you exactly how "you" are responding to life and to others, and ultimately what is the focus of your inner world. To the degree that you have explored the depths of yourself will you be able to recognize your inner patterns reflected to you thru another human being's behavior. This mirror exemplifies the universal principle of "like attracts like" in exactness, as well as "opposites attract." Our outer world always reflects our inner vibration.

This is always the first mirror to be addressed as any Being of Light begins the ascension process into Christhood. It is the most difficult mirror to fully acknowledge and accept, for the alter-ego is a master at projecting onto another something you don't like or refuse to acknowledge about yourself. The aspirant will not be able to advance in the evolutionary spiral of Self consciousness until this mirror is fully recognized and understood. Every other step depends upon it.

It is paramount that every individual take a full inventory of his/her motives, judgments, prejudices, fears, control issues, core beliefs, and areas of focused observation to determine the mirroring status in every relationship. This inventory is easily accessible through asking this question; "Is there anything within me that motivates me to behave in a similar fashion as the one who stands before me?" Revelation will be given to you in direct proportion to the purity of your heart's desire to know the truth about yourself.

When you find that same pattern of behavior in yourself that you no longer desire to be drawn into your life via another relationship encounter, ask for assistance in the transformation of the perceived reality that impulses that behavior, and the thought and feeling behind it. Then, surrender it to your I AM Spirit Self. Always remember to solicit the I AM of your Twin Soul as well. This is powerful in the acceleration of aligning consciousness with eternal Truth.

The law of *attraction* is responding in alignment with your energy vibration, whether that be positive or negative. It attracts, it multiplies, it increases. God's precious law always deals with increase, more not less, and it is indifferent to *what* is increased. What happens is, as you think about something or give your inner attention to it, you emit a vibration that matches whatever it is that you are observing or thinking. Then the universe, which operates on the law of *attraction*, responds to your vibration attracting whatever is the focus. It's like a radio signal that you are outputting. As you vibrationally output it, sometimes from a conscious level and sometimes from an unconscious level, the universe receives that signal at your point of attraction and then matches it with exactness. That is how everything in your experience comes to you. It's a vibrational response or match to what you are vibrationally outputting. It makes no difference whether you are observing something, coming to a decision about something, believing in something, or remembering or imagining something; you are offering a vibrational output which will be matched.

The thing that you most truly desire is to be in vibrational match with your Source energy, or God essence, and the goodness that essence promises in manifestation. You rarely, if ever, however, become a perfect vibrational match to your desire, because contained within you is the memory of the contrast of your true desire. Many of you are well into the idea of positive thinking, aligning your vibrations with affirmations and thoughts of goodness and good things that are the promises of the kingdom of God.   But, when you affirm something of God's good such as a loving, harmonious relationship, a new car or home, or enough money in the bank, and then in the next in-breath remember what it is like to experience lack in these areas, your focus of energy identifies with what you don't want, and the universe, by the law of attraction, seeks to match that thought in manifestation. Without contrast you would not be able to come to new choices for greater good, and from that viewpoint contrast is a good thing. However, the contrast that is essential to coming to any decision is more than likely the contrast that binds you to the opposite of your true desire. In trying to alleviate the unwanted thing from your life, somehow, early on in your experience, you became convinced that when you see something you do not want, you must push what you do not want away to leave room for what you do want. The law of attraction says, the more you push, the more focused energy you give to the unwanted, and the universe, which is no respecter of vibrations and which doesn't understand exclusion, seeks only to do what is true to its nature, and that is bring that very thing unto you. With this understanding, you can clearly see how you can truly desire one thing but draw to yourself the exact opposite with any energy that puts focus on elimination of the unwanted. This is one view of the law of attraction from the understanding that, just as like attracts like, opposites attract.

A deeper focus into the principle of this first mirror reveals this great truth: "Opposites attract *because* like attracts like." Very often you will be fully focused on the *ideal* from every position within you. By "position" we mean you are affirming the ideal, thinking about the ideal, emotionally excited about the ideal, feeling the ideal, etc. Memory of the contrast has become so faint it no longer carries enough energy to emit a vibration from you which resonates with it. But, as you look out into your life you become aware you have drawn just the opposite of what you are deeply focused on. How can this be if like attracts like? Very simply stated, your higher frequency vibration of the good attracts everything unlike itself into your higher vibration to be lifted by it! Many students of metaphysics become confused or discouraged by this truth, but, when understood from the continual expansion of Grace consciousness within us, it becomes the most exciting aspect of the law of attraction. If you are truly holding only the imprint of the greater good within you, trust if something less than that imprint appears in your life, the universal law of Grace is attracting the lesser vibration to the higher one to transmute that vibration and bring it into the collective expression of the greater God consciousness.

We see this aspect of the law of Grace at work in relationships and events around the world in growing numbers because the increased vibrational attunement of consciousness to the Love of God is now drawing everything unlike itself to the surface. In business, management positions at the top are filled with people who have the greatest capacity to resolve conflict and bring resolution through their focus on harmony, love and wisdom. Yet, they are the ones that are always drawing fires into their offices to be put out. In greater numbers, children with traumatic cellular memory at the soul level are being drawn to parents with the greatest capacity of patience and unconditional love. This is happening in reverse as well. Children of very high vibrational energy are being born into low energy environments. Even Mother Earth is responding with upheaval and chaos as the consciousness of love and peace becomes more and more the collective of humanity. She is giving birth to a new earth as we bring down heaven from above, and everything unlike heaven that has been collected in the cellular memory of our beloved planet is being eliminated.

It is important as you continue to stand before the focus of this mirror not to get discouraged or dismayed at what you see. Nor must you try to discern whether your inner posture is askew or whether it is the one who stands before you. It matters not whether you are the one who has manifested the undesirable or whether the one before you is seeking to come up higher. The only thing that is important, in either case, is the re-membering of your vibration to Source in any given moment, for that is what changes the picture in the mirror and creates for you, and the one looking back at you, a new world. Thus, the grand design for the continual evolution of consciousness progresses by the miraculous law of Grace which always deals with the increase of God consciousness through the alignment of your vibration to love.

We include here the "Grace Prayer" that has proven to be the Grace-full way to have these hidden agendas transformed by the I AM Presence. We encourage you to repeat it daily, many times. It will be a catalyst for the activation of spiritual energy that will "heal you at depth" that you may truly glorify your God Self and open to the conscious vibration of Truth that will set you free. Your Twin Soul will also benefit from your use of this prayer.

The
Grace Prayer

For Thee I Thirst.
Into Thy hands I commit my Spirit,
(My soul, my body, my life, or any error perception)

Thy Will is my Will.
Thy Will be done through me now!
Heal me at depth.

Reveal that which needs to be revealed.
Heal that which needs to be healed,
(In other words, Father forgive them...the patterns
for they know not what they do)
That I may glorify You, God, "I AM"
And live in the consciousness of Grace.

It is finished!

Mirror Number Two:
The Mirror of Your
Resistance
(Your judgmental charge)

If we completely understood the principle at the core of the first mirror of attraction, and were able to align ourselves with it in all its reflections, we would be living a life of Truth and the alter-ego would not be able to present its face. It would be recognized for what it is ... an illusion of consciousness out of vibrational harmony with Truth. But, that is not the case for most of us, and so it is necessary that we rend the veil of illusion through the application of wisdom and love by looking deeper into the one mirror of Self through the second mirror, the Mirror of Your Resistance. This is a very clouded mirror at first and only comes into focus when the images of the first mirror are windexed daily.

Once you clean up the patterns of behavior that are the effects of deep seeded core beliefs which are not in alignment with Truth, you will most likely shift your pattern from (a) *doing* what you used to behold another doing that you don't like, to (b) *seeing* in another something you used to do but would no longer do. For example: Let's say in looking closely at yourself through first mirror reflection, you discovered that you were constantly being criticized because you actually focused your vibration in finding fault with others, even if not verbalized. This resulted in drawing into your life those who found fault with you and most of your efforts. You have prayed for this pattern of mind to be transformed so that you no longer have the need to do such an ungodly thing, and you have succeeded to a great degree by focusing only on the good in all. Now, however, your emotional buttons get pushed every time you see someone else criticizing another. You would no longer do this, and it really gets to you that others still do it. You have mastered the error behavior, but you have not forgiven the judgment around that behavior, and very subtly that has become the focus of your attention. Now your vibration is in alignment with your resistance to the old behavior pattern that used to be in you, and you find yourself attracting that behavior into your life via another. Actually, the resistance re-establishes resonance with the old vibration and registers in your body/mind/spirit (it registers in your bones first) attracting that same energy to you and affecting your manifest world.

It is important to remember that the subconscious level of soul is the storehouse of all thoughts, feelings and emotions. It does not have the capacity to discern when a thought is directly related to self or to another. It simply records the feeling and the emotion, and through the law of correspondence it will draw into your life, or create for you, the very thing on which you have the greatest judgment or you most resist. Your manifest experience will always be directly reflective of the emotional charge you have about anything, for the law of attraction continues to hold true in alignment with your vibration.

Aspirants will often approach this reflective mirror with the question to Self: "What is it in my consciousness that is drawing this to me?" In the frantic search, for the life of them, they can't find anything that resembles the behavior of that which is showing up. When this is the revelation, it is time to look deeper to see if you have any judgmental emotion attached to something. If you do not acknowledge this, it will keep you in a sense of victimization and will not permit you to rise above the pawn of karma which continually draws into your life that upon which you have a charge.

Many of you have a big thing about control and freedom. For many years you have been working on releasing your need to control, knowing this will free you and the ones you are trying to control. You have really done a pretty good job. You pride yourself in giving your children your support as they make their choices in life. You feel very good about no longer needing to have others believe exactly like you do. If you don't get your way about something, you don't go bananas any more. Good for you. You've made wonderful progress. But, what transpires within your soul when someone tries to control you or someone you love? How do you feel about controlling people? I'll bet you're pretty good at spotting manipulators, aren't you? Um Hum! You see, the energetic emotion (energy in motion) that is released in you when you see a characteristic in others that you really have a charge on, is very similar to the emotion that was released when you used to have a need to do the same thing. Your original need to control was your alter-ego's way of making you think you were protected from other controlling people. Alter-ego logic surmised that in order not to be controlled, you had to control first. The only thing this really accomplished was the generation of more controlling circumstances and people in your life. Like attracts like. Because you have not made peace with, or freed yourself from, the need to pass judgment on those who control, you are still drawing controlling situations into your life. This is a very subtle movement of mind and must be closely monitored in order to detect it. The alter-ego will also jump to the front lines with its illusionary reasoning that you are most justified in your judgment, and that your judgment will somehow correct their error behavior or impulse you into an action that will. Think again. The great cosmic law of Grace states; "you cannot solve the problem on the level of the problem--you must rise above it." You only perpetuate the problem by the intensity of your energy in resistance to it. Your vibration of resistance is a perfect match to the very thing you desire to eliminate.

Sometime, during the course of the eternal journey, you will be required to relinquish *ALL* judgment. This is the most difficult hurdle for the mind to surmount. In your sense of separation, judgment has motivated your patterns of behavior that have kept you in a false sense of protection. Judgment is a survival mechanism for the alter-ego.

It is important to note there is a big difference between judgment and discernment. Judgment releases negative degenerative energy that is harmful and destructive in vibration. Discernment is the gift of Spirit that impulses divine action. When the alter-ego is no longer in charge, discernment will flow through the soul with its purest evaluation and impulse right action.

What ultimately is occurring here? The soul is giving birth to a forgotten memory of the Superconscious Self. It is the memory of Compassion. True Compassion is the highest expression of love that is free from judgment and emotion of a degenerative nature. It is the call from Spirit to see through Its eyes. It is the ability to *allow* all things while, at the same time, being open to Divine impulse to right action. True Compassion is the capacity to experience true feelings without distortion.

The following definition is excerpted from Gregg Braden's materials for his intensive seminar entitled *Walking Between the Worlds, The Science of Compassion.* © 1995 *Sacred Spaces/Ancient Wisdom:*

"Compassion" may be defined as "Emotion" without charge, "Thought" without attachment to the outcome and "Feeling" without distortion.

*Compassion allows the ability to view the events and actions of life for the purity of what they are as opposed to the judgments that your experienced fear placed upon them. In Compassion, there can be no right, no wrong, no good, no bad. There simply "is" and there is the consequences of choice.

*As earth moves rapidly toward the "Shift of the Ages," you are asked to demonstrate your mastery of emotion, thought and resultant feelings as your ability to accommodate tremendous change in your life.

*You are asked to transcend polarity (Good, evil, right, wrong, light, dark) while still living within the polarity! This is not an insignificant task!

Compassion is your highest expression of love!

Compassion as a "Response"

☆Through Compassion you will never see a "right", "wrong", "good" or bad.

☆You will recognize masterful beings experiencing the outcome of their creations.

☆What you "do" is less important than what you "become" in the moment of your opportunity.

☆Through Compassion you will determine the highest response, appropriate for yourself, in a given situation, in a given moment.

With the birth of Compassion as the new realized state of consciousness, you become free of all thoughts, feelings and emotions that bind your soul in a low vibration. True Compassion draws your awareness into the present moment and empowers you to make choices anchored in Truth vs. judgment. The subconscious becomes an open receiver, free for the first time to impress pure thought vibration upon the canvas of the conscious mind.

To assist you in moving from judgment into Compassion, we offer this simple exercise to help you pinpoint where you are leaking judgmental energy. Ask yourself what it is that you pride yourself in the most. The opposite of that soul quality, when expressed by others, will usually trigger your charge issues. For example, are you patient? If so, how do you feel about impatient people? Are you open-minded? How do you feel about narrow-minded people? Do you always give people the benefit of the doubt? Then, is it hard for you to deal with people who always look for the worst in others? Can you embrace several schools of thought?

What do you feel when someone tries to proselyte you? Do you respect others' privacy and space? Does your button get pushed when you receive unsolicited telephone calls? Are you a courteous driver? What goes through your mind when you encounter bullies on the road?

Take time to engage the next exercise. It will be well worth your while in understanding yourself and why you still keep drawing certain experiences and relationships into your life. Your emotional charges will keep you suspended in the abyss of social consciousness and forever tied to the bucking horse.

My Pride and My Prejudice

That which I pride myself in the most:	My most judgmental charge:
1.	
2.	
3.	
4.	
5.	
6.	
7.	
8.	
9.	
10.	
11.	
12.	

Because of the perfect mirror of Twin Soul relationships, your most judgmental charges will be activated by the driving force of love that is propelling the reunion forward. Love calls forth everything unlike itself, to be transformed into itself. In the presence of Love there is NO judgment ... NONE! Are you willing and ready to let all judgment go? If you are not, you are not ready for the Twin Soul relationship or for the fulfillment of your true desires.

It will behoove you to become pure in heart and ask yourself the following questions:

1.   Am I willing to release all judgments, or are there a few I am justified to keep?

2.   Am I willing to accept full responsibility for my life, or are there some areas where I still believe myself to be the victim?

3.   Am I willing to risk loving, regardless of the consequences?

If you can say "yes" to all three of these questions, you are ready for the birth of Compassion and worthy (by right of consciousness) to experience the inflow of Grace in alignment with your Christ vibration. Your daily bread of leftover negative karma will immediately find a black hole in time, and you will enter through the portal of the kingdom of heaven to be lavished with a banquet table of Grace.

Mirror Number Three:

The Mirror of Your Desire

(That which you sense has been lost, given away, taken away, or you never had)

Desire at the current level of awareness, for most of us, is a yearning for that which we perceive we do not have. If we could instantly awaken to the Truth, we would see that we could have everything we possibly desire at this very instant if we were in vibrational harmony with our true Self. If we could bring all of consciousness to "BEING" in vibrational harmony with our inner Source in the present moment, the kingdom of heaven would be at hand. Until that moment occurs, we will draw relationships and situations into our lives that reflect back to us either the seemingly unattainable fulfillment or lack of those things we desire, because our vibration is centered on the idea, "I don't have access to what I want."

The opposite spectrum of desiring what we don't have is desiring not to lose, have stolen or have taken away that which we do have. Both of these perspectives constitute the makeup of desire, and at the core of each perception is the *fear* of loss or lack. The universe operates on one law and one law only: the law of attraction. There is no such thing as the law of lack. The universe is always creating more in direct alignment with the focus of consciousness in relationship to any given thing. If we desire more abundance, and focus on abundance, abundance will be attracted to us. If we desire more abundance and focus on lack, *more* lack will be attracted to us-- not less, *more!* The mind which desires from the vibrational belief that it does not have what it wants attracts *more,* not less, of what it doesn't want. Universal law is oblivious as to *what* is attracted. It never produces less of anything. Remember, the universe does not understand exclusion. It only understands inclusion. God is all inclusive, not exclusive. That is why what we resist persists, and why what we try to eliminate from our lives we increase.

Look closely again at all you desire and you will see that your desires are anchored in a fear of *lack, loss,* or *not enough.* All fears are based on this perception when taken to their core; even the universal ones such as the fear of abandonment or separation, the fear of death, the fear of being unworthy, the fear of not enough, and the fear of disease. Abandonment and separation imply *exclusion;* fear of death implies *absence* of life; not worthy implies *not* good *enough;* fear of disease implies *absence* of ease and *lack* of health. Therefore, as you allow yourself to focus clearly on all your desires, you will uncover your most deeply hidden fear of *loss.* But remember: *God, and God functioning in God's universe does not know loss. God only knows increase...more!* This makes all your fears unfounded as well as out of vibrational harmony with *more* of the very thing you want.

Be willing to look more deeply into yourself now by examining your desires to see where you have pushed the very thing you desire away from you *OR attracted into your life in someone else the very thing you feel you no longer have, want to have or are afraid of losing.* This is the magnetic field of attraction that most new relationships are founded upon. Each individual sees in the other individual that which they think they either lost, had taken away, gave away or never had. We know a young man who met a woman and immediately got in touch with what it was about her that attracted him. It was her sense of innocence. Later he found himself weeping as he touched that spot in his soul memory that felt as though he had *lost* his sense of innocence due to the wisdom he had gained through his experiences of life.

In a recent workshop a couple shared with us that when they met, the man was immediately attracted to his partner's playfulness and child-like spontaneity, while the woman was attracted to his depth of wisdom and maturity. Both felt each was reflecting something he or she had never had! The man grew up in a very strict household where hard work and no play was the norm. The woman, in childhood, was never validated for her wisdom and cleverness. In both of these examples the relationships grew into deep love for one another for the first year. At the end of the first year, or honeymoon period, however, the deep sense of loss that each felt became their focus, and the anger and resentment they felt in their sense of loss within themselves came to the surface creating conflict and dissatisfaction in the relationship. It was not until they both realized they were perfect mirrors for the other's illusion of loss or lack that they began to heal. And they did so by embracing the *more* in their partners which called forth that same said nature within them. God does not deal in loss, but in the increase of the nature of God's Self in all. We can never give away, lose, have taken away, or not have anything that is true of the nature of God, for we are created in God's image likeness. We can only increase whatever we attract to us by our vibration.

To help clear the focus on this mirror, take a reality check in your mind of your heart's desires. Make a list of them. Grab a sheet of paper and simply begin listing things you "want." Your list of items will most likely fit into one of these categories: (1) a material object that costs money or is unobtainable for whatever reason; (2) a soul quality aspiration; (3) healing of a mental, emotional or physical condition; (4) change in relationships; and/or (5) life achievements.

Beside each "want" item, identify which of these categories your desire seems to fit. Does the "want" item reflect something you feel you have never had, lost, gave away or had taken away? Now, see if you can make a correlation to help you identify your fears of loss and see them for the illusions they are, thus opening your mind and heart to a tremendous shift of consciousness in the concept of desire. Instead of seeing desire as *yearning for something you do not have, rather see it as the impulse from your true nature to accept what is already and always has been yours.*

The chart on the next page will assist you in completing this exercise and prepare you to address your greatest fears through the truth revealed in the next mirror.

The Mirror of Your Desire

My Desire:	Category	Belief	Core Fear

	(1) Material object
	(2) Soul aspiration
	(3) Healing
	(4) Change
	(5) Life achievement
	(6) Other
		(1) Never had
		(2) Lost
		(3) Had taken away
		(4) Gave away
			(1) Abandonment
			    or separation
			(2) Not worthy or
			    good enough
			(3) Surrender/trust
			(4) Other

1.			
2.			
3.			

Once you have identified your desires, which category they fit, the core belief and the core fear, you will begin to see "why" the desires elude you. They rest in a deep rooted belief that generates an emotion of fear at the subjective level of consciousness. That which you fear has now come upon you as the experience of either a "lack" of what you want or "too much" of what you don't want in your life.

These core fears are expressed as certain behavior patterns, which we will address in the next mirror. As these behavior patterns are acted out, they draw to you relationships and experiences that mirror more of what you fear. There is no way around it. You draw into your life the exact reflection of your core belief, and the more you participate in the behavior pattern that prevents resolution of the fear, the more you separate yourself from the possibility of manifesting your desire.

Look closely at all desires. Within them you will see your greatest fears and beliefs that are rooted in the error perception of an eternal life principle, for they present to the mind the concept that you don't have and can't get what you want.

We are constantly looking to our relationships and outer situations to fill the empty space this type of desiring creates. They can never do this for us, and that is why we are always disappointed in people and events that don't provide for us what we think we "want." This will always cause us to project our judgment onto another person and feel deeply frustrated when they don't give us what we need.

Mirror Number Four

The Mirror of Your Fear

(Your Most Forgotten Truth)

As we learned in the previous mirror, fears are not in vibrational harmony with our Source or our true nature. The law of attraction does not distinguish between our fears and our desires. The Universe responds to that which we focus our attention upon. To fear anything is to focus upon it, especially if the fear is charged emotionally. Even though we may want only harmony in our lives and do everything within our power to bring that about, a deep-seated fear of disharmony or conflict will draw or attract to us even greater opportunities to experience that which we fear. The more we experience the disharmony, the more amplified is the fear and the emotion attached to it, and a degenerative cycle results.

The only way to break the cycle and free ourselves from the consequences of our fears is to face them and see them for what they are -- illusions, masking from us forgotten truths and our greatest potential gifts. It is essential to the process, however, to recognize that the path to identification of and confrontation with our core fears is somewhat indirect, thanks to our alter-ego's tactic of creating behavioral patterns through which it seeks to avoid the experience of that which we fear.

As an example, as a child we may have experienced the repeated anger or even rage of a parent directed at us which we associated with rejection. We interpreted the behavior as an indication that we were not "worthy" or "good enough." Over time, we learned how to avoid confrontations and rejections, such as through not expressing our real feelings, not discussing our opinions, throwing our own anger fit, or going into hiding whenever the behavior started to surface. We also developed an early warning system to alert us to the potential onset of the behavior to be avoided -- typically a "feeling" of tenseness in the pit of the stomach or solar plexus.

Our learned behavioral patterns of adolescence usually carry over into adulthood. In our example, we may, as an adult, continue to avoid expressing our true feelings and/or get very tense whenever the "feeling" arises or we sense the onset of some act of rejection. Any expressed anger by another is immediately registered as threatening and as rejection of us. Ironically, for those in relationship with us, our protective behavior is often viewed by them as withdrawal, aloofness, indifference, or even rejection on our part. It may even draw anger from the other person, thereby re-confirming to us the validity of our fear. In other words, the behavioral patterns developed early in our lives unintentionally draw to us the very thing we seek to escape. We often fail to recognize that it is our own behavioral patterns which are actually feeding our fears, because we have disassociated those behavioral patterns from the core fears which gave birth to them. We have developed habitual behavior patterns which seem to have a life of their own, and we feel hopeless and helpless.

The truth is that we are, and always have been, "worthy." While we may have been the recipient or seeming "victim" of the expressed anger of another, the source of the anger was within the other person. Rather than being rejected, something that we did or failed to do triggered in the other person a feeling that they were powerless, not respected, not loved, etc. Irrespective of whatever may have triggered it and however disguised, anger is an emotional response to a perceived threat and a call for love. If the anger is recognized for what it truly is, it could be responded to with compassion rather than with resistance, thereby disarming the one feeling threatened and making it safe for both parties to break the behavioral pattern. Unfortunately, however, those on the receiving end of anger or disgust tend to see it as a form of rejection or attack, rather than for what it really is, and they therefore go into a protective and often emotional state of resistance to the behavior. The resistance feeds the fear of the other person, and the mirroring effect kicks in, intensifying and amplifying the fears and emotions of both parties until one or the other can "break" the cycle -- usually resulting from an emotional breakdown or physical separation -- leaving one or both persons feeling emotionally "injured," thereby reinforcing the fears and further fueling the habitual, debilitating process.

The pain we experience is directly proportional to the degree of our unwillingness to face our fears (or to resolve them by remembering the Truth). The habitual behavior developed to protect ourselves from the pain of these Friday Night Fright Shows pushes us ever deeper into our illusions (and further from our forgotten Truth).

Innumerable examples can be given of these cycles of degenerative behavior which arise from our unfounded or illusory fears. It is important to recognize that our core fears are the fuel that sustains the alter-ego. In addition to our unloving behavior patterns, our core fears perpetuate inharmony, disease, lack, judgmental thoughts, and all addictions. In order to face our particular fears and recognize that which they are mirroring to us, it is first important to recognize what is at the core of all fear.

At the core of all fear we find consciousness standing before a mirror that reflects "nothing," which in our current reality check represents the "unknown." Within the unknown there is no point of reference upon which to place our identity. Thus, our identity feels threatened. Yet, at the core of all life is the impulse to embrace more life, or more of the unknown. Such is the nature of consciousness, because it is ever expanding in awareness. Consciousness awakening to unlimited Self feels very threatened when it cannot see beyond its current point of reference, so it feels fearful.

In the absolute of Self, all is known. We are a paradox unto ourself, however, in that we are the knower, the known and the "knowing." We perceive ourself to be in hot pursuit of all that can be known through our evolution of "knowing" or learning as we seek to make contact with the infinite Knower. And, yet, we are THAT, all of THAT. We ARE the Knower, the known and the knowing.

In the process of becoming realized in this state of Being, consciousness is drawn in upon itself in pursuit of a greater knowingness of itself. As it does this, it brings along with it the collective "conscious" understanding it has gathered through many evolutions in life. In order to expand the boundaries of our boundless Self, we are asked, by the impulse of divine life, to be willing to "leave the Father's house" (that state of consciousness which is known) and explore the infinite kingdom of God consciousness that is our divine inheritance.

To the alter-ego, this invitation looks like being asked to embark into unknown worlds and unfamiliar territory through which it might lose its identity altogether. But, the truth of the matter is, that territory represents the familiar womb of God from which we emerged. We have been and always will be one with the "unknown," the Truth that sets us free to be more of what we were created to be.

In the beginning, we existed in a state of consciousness that didn't know it knew. So, in a very real sense, our awakening can be likened to waking up from the amnesia of eternal life. We are remembering what we knew without knowing that we knew. Each fear, then, will masquerade some glorious Truth we have, in essence, forgotten.

In Truth, we don't fear the unknown at all, but rather we have some memory of a past experience which we project onto the present moment. Our fears are the overlays the alter-ego has placed upon the soul (entire spectrum of awareness) in its journey to remembering. They are not based on any eternal principle of Truth, for within them there is no Truth. They are perceptions of consciousness we have gathered in our efforts to awaken in a polarized existence. In other words, they are the effects of judgments we have placed upon that which we have manifested in awakening our creative potential through the Tree of the Knowledge of Good and Evil. Our wisdom texts tell us this has been a good thing, but the greater commandment is to awaken by partaking of the Tree of Life in which there is no good or evil, there just IS! We are asked to transcend the consciousness of polarity while still existing in polarity. This is not an easy task and can only be done when there is no judgment. *All fears are the result of our judgments anchored in the core of the unremembered.*

The process of learning our lessons through remembrance of our forgotten Truth must begin with identifying our protective behavioral patterns of resistance. Simply ask yourself, "how do I cope with my fear of _____ (name it)?" "What are my reactions every time I feel _____?" As noted, your pattern of behavior becomes habitual making you feel so removed from your fear that you don't even recognize it. It is very important to become conscious of any emotion or feeling that is something less than peace, love or joy, for that provides the opportunity to remember your most forgotten Truth and free yourself from some deeply rooted illusion. This is the real process of spiritual evolution. To the degree you are free, happy and "in" love, you are advancing on your spiritual path. Staying locked into fear patterns is stagnation at its best and degeneration at its worst.

Once you have identified your key behavioral patterns, you should be able to pinpoint the core fears from which you are seeking to escape. Each core fear is a mirror of a forgotten Truth you are being asked to remember. The key is to not dwell upon or seek to overcome the illusory fear, but rather to *identify with the Truth veiled by it.*

Forgotten Truth usually becomes remembered by degrees. At first much of what you are seeking to know will be held as a mental concept. It may take a lot of focus, one-pointed vision and intention to fully remember and *know.* Your objective is to move your understanding from an intellectual perception of Truth into the heart of *knowing* it!

In order to assist you in recognizing your forgotten Truth and anchoring it into your heart, we include the exercises on the following pages. In addition, to assit you in realizing your Truth, we offer a technique called "Radio Star." "Radio Star" is an acronym for a process of mind/heart intention. It is the prelude to the "Star System" that will be introduced in Mirror Number 7.

Radio Star!

(A cosmic radio source of very small dimensions and relatively strong radiation.)   *Webster*

R   Recognize any inharmonious energy as a Star signal for the gift of Truth that is seeking to make itself known.

A   Ask for assistance from your Spirit, the Spirit of your Twin Soul and the Spirit of all beings of the Light of Truth.

D   Declare your pure heart's intention.

I   Identify with the Truth: That aspect of the nature of God within which is omnipresent NOW!

O   Om...Claim "I AM Om-Aum!"

S   Surrender
T   Trust
A   Allow
R   Rest

My Most Forgotten Truth

Behavior Pattern	Mirrored Fear	My Forgotten Truth
1.		
2.		
3.		
4.		
5.		
6.		
7.		
8.		
9.		

Remembered Truth

*Your greatest fear suppresses your most
forgotten Truth!*

*Your alter-ego behavior pattern creates
exactly the <u>opposite</u>
of that which you desire most in your life!*

*Recognized alter-ego behavior patterns
provide you the opportunity to identify
your greatest fears
(Your most forgotten Truth),
so that you no longer drive from your life the
very things that are most precious to you.**

---

* *Adapted from materials for Gregg Braden's intensive seminar <u>Walking Between the Worlds,
The Science of Compassion</u>. © 1995 Sacred Spaces/Ancient Wisdom.*

When Truth is remembered at the conscious level it establishes a vibratory resonance field that serves as a magnetic attractor of the eternal Truth which is at all times resonating at the Superconscious or Spirit level of mind within you. Here we have that law of attraction again. When the conscious and Superconscious are in resonance, this state of mind draws everything unlike it into the higher state. In this way, all that is contained as subconscious memory which is not in alignment with Truth becomes exposed by the light of Truth and thus becomes the Truth. Those memories which are not the Truth of your being may never be revealed to you but simply transmuted or alchemied by the Truth being held at conscious and Superconscious levels of mind. This is the way of transformation by Grace.

It is of the utmost importance then for you to be ever conscious of your belief system and what you know to be the Truth that sets you free. Take time to identify your belief system based upon what you know to be the eternal Truths of God. Then, hold these Truths to be self evident as you progress through the awakening stages of these mirrors.

We have included a list of our personal beliefs regarding what we consider to be the eternal Truths of God. You may not agree with ours, but that doesn't matter. What matters is that you awaken to the Truth that resides within you. The greatest Truth of all is that whatever Truth you hold will become true for you.

This I Believe!
(Principles of Eternal Life)

1. _____

2. _____

3. _____

4. _____

5. _____

6. _____

7. _____

8. _____

9. _____

10. _____

This We Believe!

1.   There is only one Presence and one Power, God the good...Omnipotence, Omniscience and Omnipresence!

2.   Life is CONSCIOUSNESS & Energy manifesting in alignment with the Law of Cause and Effect and its fulfilment, GRACE!

3.   LIFE IS ETERNAL.

4.   I am ONE with all Life.

5.   Every experience is an opportunity to demonstrate mastery in unconditional love.

6.   ALL things work together for GOOD!

7.   The purpose of life is to KNOW GOD as I AM & become a conscious co-creator.

8.   I AM created in the image and likeness of God. God's nature is my nature.

9.   There are no coincidences.

10.   LOVE IS ALL THERE IS!

Mirror Number Five
The Mirror of Your Quest
(What you came to learn as your potential gift)

Each of us intuitively knows we are on a quest of learning. Earth has very often been referred to as a school by many enlightened Beings. If we do not understand the purpose of that learning, it can feel as though we are struggling for naught, *indeed*.

This Sacred Mirror helps us understand the great gift that awaits as we gaze into the reflection of our life lessons. That which seems to be a constant struggle for us to overcome contains within it an important lesson to be mastered, reflecting our most forgotten truth and our greatest potential gift. In spiritual evolution, these lessons always deal with "soul" qualities that are being drawn into alignment with the eternal Self; soul qualities of God's divine nature of the deeply embedded truth of Being within us. As these soul qualities mature, they then come forth into expression as our talents, gifts, careers and highest modes of expression.

This mirror underlies the previous mirror to reveal the association of our life lessons to the resolution of our fears and alter-ego behavior patterns. It also helps us get in touch with the relationship of our life lessons to our potential gifts. As we have seen, our behavior patterns often mask our core fears which, in turn, veil our most forgotten Truths. Remembrance of our most forgotten Truths reveals to us our life lessons. Our life lessons, in turn, hold the key to obtaining that which we most seek -- the *Holy Grail* of our individual spiritual quest.

In compliance with divine law, we see that the law of attraction will draw relationships and circumstances into our lives that mirror for us and give us the opportunity to master our lessons. Since we are the microcosm of the macrocosmic God, the impulse to know and express the perfection of our divine nature never ceases. We are destined to become the full expression of all the qualities of the nature of God. That is why we will continue to feel like we are taking the same course over and over again, addressing the same issues although perhaps with new people, until the soul quality is mastered. If you thought you had mastered "patience," for instance, but really hadn't, believe us when we say, the universe will provide you with an opportunity to check out your progress.

What also is revealed in this mirror is, that which we admire the most in others is reflective of a soul quality we are seeking to have fully realized in ourselves. Often, however, we will have a very strange reaction to people we draw into our life who express the qualities we most admire. That quality will sometimes turn us completely off. For example: lets say you are learning "truth needs no defense," yet you keep observing that you are constantly feeling compelled to defend yourself. You may draw someone into your life who has mastered this soul quality and simply has no need to argue with you. Because your viewpoint is different from theirs, and because you haven't mastered this soul quality, you will get angry because they won't argue back. Of course, the opposite may also happen. You may draw someone who, like you, is still very defensive. Like attracts like, but, remember, it is also true that opposites attract, because like attracts like. Let us explain again. The one who has mastered patience is attracted to the one who hasn't mastered it, because that soul quality in the master is calling forth that same soul quality (though hidden) in the aspirant. Patience is attracting patience (the divine soul quality), but in so doing draws forth everything unlike itself. These examples are the two properties of the law of attraction in soul development.

Mastery of your lessons is not accomplished by focusing upon your shortcomings for, as we have learned, to do that is to perpetuate them. Our lesson is never to "not" do anything. Resistance (fear, judgment, etc.) only feeds the negative behavior patterns and attracts more of that resisted. Our purpose, and whether we are prepared to acknowledge it or not our heart's desire, is to embody and freely express those soul qualities inherent within us reflective of the true nature of God. To the extent we are bottled up in resistance, we are withholding ourselves -- our greatest gift -- and we are denying ourselves our heart's desire.

It is important that we get in touch with that which we "love" to do. We "love" to do that which is in the flow of life free from resistance of any kind. Stated differently, to be "in love" is to be in a non-resistant state of being in alignment with the true nature of who we are -- our heart's desire. That is the *Holy Grail* of our quest, and it leads us to our mission and purpose in this incarnation. The map to the *Holy Grail* thus starts with our "issues," which reflect our lessons, which reveal those soul qualities in alignment with our true nature, which are expressed through doing that which we "love" to do, which is our mission and purpose -- the fulfillment of our heart's desire.

When we are doing what we love to do, the divine nature of God's consciousness flows freely through us. The more we identify with doing what we love, the more the nature of God occupies consciousness, and the law of attraction serves to transform soul quality lessons into spiritual gifts. Doing what you love to do cannot be emphasized enough as a tool for accelerated spiritual advancement. This practice will always lead you into the fullness of your mission and purpose for this incarnation.

As we begin to look deeply into this mirror, we offer a list of examples of the soul qualities associated with the nature of God. This gives us the courses in life that we are all asked to master, for they are inherent within our own soul. Add to the list any aspects of God's nature you feel we have left out that may be reflective of your individual life lessons. Then turn to the worksheet and begin.

God's Divine Nature Is:

Love	Faith	Strength	Power
Patient	Order	Allowing	Joy
Wisdom	Tolerant	Forgiving	Peace
Inclusive	Nonresistant	Willing	Defenseless
Beauty	Steadfast	Empowering	Boundless
Devoted	Enduring	Compassion	Opulent

The following chart is designed to help you grasp the depth of this mirror and become more fully conscious. It also should help you to see that your relationships are your greatest blessing, offering to you the opportunity to become free in the glorified state of your God-given potential. Always remember that it is not your destiny to be chained to the never-ending karmic wheel, but rather to drink of the cup of boundless and eternal life.

The Mirror of Your Quest

Life's Constant Issues	Lessons or Soul Quality Being Mastered	I Love to do this...

First, see if you can find a parallel between your life's constant issues and the lessons or soul qualities being mastered. Then, determine what you love to do the most. Apply what you love to do in as much of your day as possible. Your soul qualities will begin to emerge as mastered gifts transforming your life's issues into lessons learned and ultimately revealing your mission.

With this and every mirror, it is important to keep in mind that, if you have drawn your Twin into your life, all mirrors will be completely transparent. Nothing can remain hidden in the presence of the Light, and you and your Twin are, in the absolute, pure Light. Your magnetic fields are the most identical of any two human beings on the planet. You will reflect the absolute of every cosmic law. Each of you will feel totally exposed, because you are. Your lessons will go into acceleration, as will the expression of your gifts. The Twin relationship can be *very* intense. At the same time, however, the opportunity for growth and mastery is exponentially increased.

Mirror Number Six

The Mirror of Your Mastery

(Your Self Remembered)

There are many gifts and talents which you are expressing in the world at this time. Yet, you have been so bent on the "issues" and lessons you came to learn, you may have overlooked those gifts and talents. They are the accumulated alignments you have already attained through many lifetimes of experience. It is important to recognize and acknowledge these gifts, for they are the cornerstones of consciousness that empower you to embrace even more of yourself. They also are collectives or enhancers that add brilliance, polish and shine to your current mission and world service. The more you identify with them, the more they will be integrated into every aspect of consciousness.

The ability to recognize and embrace your gifts, in humble acceptance, will be a master key to moving on into the final Mirror of Oneness. So let's take a look at the Master within us, our relationships and life's experiences, to unveil, in all their glory, our gifts.

First ask yourself the question, "which of God's soul qualities is easiest for me to express?" Return to the list of God's Divine Nature (p. 68). In front of each quality ask yourself, "AM I ...... ?" Then fill in the blank with the soul nature quality. If you can say yes, you've got a match. Now, return to the list of things you love to do. Can you see how each of these gifts allows you the natural, spontaneous flow of participation in a particular expression of life? Of course, your mastered gifts will always be engaged as you enter into the joy of life. Can you see, then, how mastering your lessons is the greatest opportunity of any lifetime?

Take another look at your "lessons". All of these soul qualities up for mastery are associated by you with your life's constant "issues" and challenges. Forget the challenges, and ask yourself, "am I not _____ (name the nature) in other areas of my life"? For example, you may be learning "tolerance" associated with domineering people, but aren't you tolerant of a little child's ignorance? Remember, soul qualities are inherent. They are the true nature of each soul. They simply have been forgotten and need to be remembered. The priceless gift of this mirror is to use it to anchor the fullness of your nature into the All of your consciousness. Thus, D R O P the constant thought of the futility of the "issues" and identify with the resolutions -- those energies of tolerance that you know you can express. For instance, think about the tolerance you have for the innocent child and transfer that memory; overlay it onto your life's issue. And remember, all life's issues are but innocent children which have not grown into the awareness of the Truth.

Two important aids for your are: (1) draw upon your mastered strengths to assist you in mastering those lesser qualities [Example: you are almost always open minded. Draw on the strength of your open-mindedness to help you become more tolerant. The wisdom of open-mindedness will empower your tolerance]; and (2) draw on the strength of your ability to sometimes be true to your nature in certain situations by overlaying or transferring the memory of that ability to the memory of the lesson you are in the process of learning. This is subtle, but powerful. You have built a foundation. Stand on it.

Next, think about the relationships in your life. How many people have you drawn that reflect the same gift? Many probably. They will show up in your immediate relationships, your work space, your travels, and intimate family ties. We know you also will be able to bring up folks who do not reflect these gifts. Ask yourself the question, "does their inability to express God's nature of _____ (name it) disturb me"? If you truly have mastered this soul quality, the answer will be no.

In using the Mirrors of Relationships as a tool for spiritual evolution, it is absolutely vital that you begin to IDENTIFY with the true nature of your Being. Begin to look for your mastery not only in yourself, but also in every soul you encounter. Look for it in the experiences of your life, for whatever you identify with, you become or increase.

The more you focus on this mirror by seeing God in all your relationships, the less you will focus on the previous mirrors. In this way, your gifts and talents, your mission and service work, your true spiritual Self and your Twin Soul, all will become more attracted to you.

Almost everyone has been "in love" at some time in their lives. Contemplate how you felt when you fell "in love."

Especially during the beginning of the relationship, what did it feel like for each person to only see the very best in each other, as if neither person could see any of the other person's "less than perfect" qualities? How did you respond? Do you recall the feeling of exhilaration and joy, bringing out almost childlike behavior in both? You were seeing things through "rose colored glasses," and things that normally bothered you simply rolled off your back. Dearly beloved, the experience of being "in love" is the result of mirroring the master within, as well as being in a state of complete allowance, rather than resistance. Can you imagine what it would be like to be "in love" all the time? That is where this mirror can lead you, a state of simply *"Being"* in love -- not in love "with." The state of "Being in Love" of which we speak needs no object, but it always draws unto itself that which is in resonance with the same vibration of unconditional love or that which seeks to be lifted into that vibrational frequency.

This mirror is the *turning point*. It is the beginning of the Soular Reunion into Being and approaching the New Genesis. When we stand before it, it becomes the vision that allows the "prodigal" to "come to him/her Self" -- to start the homeward journey back to the kingdom of God, remembered. It is the mirror of Alpha and Omega, the beginning and the end, and the beginning again of the true You.

As you look within yourself and within others for your Self remembered, a very subtle shift will begin to take place. You will slowly be able to see, with clarity, that which you see in another "is" yourself. That quality "is" your same said soul essence. You will begin to glimpse little fragments of de-ja-*you*! You will never be the same once you stand before this mirror on a constant basis. This is the mirror of Grace and

Truth that spirals your consciousness upward, inward, outward and far beyond into your boundless Self.

Use the chart at the end of this mirror to identify your gifts of mastery. Deeply contemplate how they are now assisting you in expressing your uniqueness. Overlay them onto your lessons to master, and, then, list everyone and everything you can possibly think of that reflects these gifts in your life right now. The keys for standing before this mirror are the same keys used for the other mirrors:

(1)   Let you heart be pure in desiring it;

(2)   Ask for assistance in recognizing it; and

(3)   Surrender to doing it!

The Mirror of Your Mastery

My Mastered Gifts	Overlay: Mastered and Inherited Gifts	Mirrored Reflections Relationships and Situations

I AM...

Mirror Number Seven

The Mirror of Your Oneness

("I AM" that "I AM")

This mirror takes the aspirant into mastery and ultimately union with the All in all, which, of course, includes your Twin Soul. It is the mirror of the "single eye" reflecting I AM "that" I AM through which the one beholding and that which is beheld become one and the same. The observer is one with the observed and the one observing. The sense of separation is no longer even a shadow, for the soul stands perfectly aligned with the Son from on high.

Once this mirror is entered, you will stand within it seeing only that which You are, looking back at You. You are one and the same. Standing before nature you will feel and know the birds' song as your own, the wind as your whispered breath, the sap in the trees as the blood that runs through your veins, the tides as the ebb and flow of your life. Judgment will be a word that has meaning no more. All of life will be allowed! Peace will be the abiding place of the soul, and freedom will be the consciousness of the boundless Self.

To draw forth the reflection of this mirror, the pure heart's intention must shift from seeking God within Self to seeking God within same said Self in Other. This is a shift that takes place at the command of the I AM Self once mystical union within individual Self has reached a certain level of integration. The spiritual quest, then, makes a 180° shift in the Soular Reunion (see the section on Soular Reunion) and becomes a conscious collective journey of remembering oneness with all Other.

This mirror is multi-dimensional and can only be viewed from within Self. Therefore, it requires that you step through its first portal by way of the unknown abyss of the STAR System. The STAR System is a state of consciousness that totally rests within itself. STAR is an acronym for:

Surrender

Trust

Allow

Rest

To enter through this portal you must have learned to take control of limited mind. In essence, what you are doing is letting go of all need for control through the power of control. Think on this; it takes a lot of control to be out of control. As consciousness begins to totally rest in the surrendered state of trust, allowing all things, the stresses and pressures that impinged upon the pituitary gland subside. This enables the pituitary gland to release hormones that bring the body and the mind into harmonic flow. This harmonic flow of energy, then, activates the pineal gland in the frontal cortex of the brain which triggers an opening in the 6th seal of consciousness drawing the aspirant into communion with Higher Mind. Higher Mind then becomes the portal through which the 7th seal of consciousness opens to reveal the connection, not only to your I AM Self, but the I AM Self in your Twin. This experience automatically shifts the journey from union with Self to union with Other Self, and the fusion in consciousness of the totality of your masculine and feminine nature in which is contained the consciousness of the All. Once this occurs, the Twin Soul consciousness is drawn through the 8th seal and begins to seek fusion in consciousness with all of humanity and, ultimately, fusion with Light Beings in all dimensions. Ah, the STAR System is vast and infinite, indeed!

There are no written exercises that can assist you in integrating this mirror. This one requires full experiential participation. Actually, it is not to be viewed at all. You must literally step through it, much like Sebastian did in the film, "The Never Ending Story." You must live it. In our mortal state, limited mind seeks to know the Truth without being required to live it. In our immortal state, all Truth must come into the experience of emotional knowingness. It is said that the longest distance the soul will travel is from the head to the heart. Your Truth must now be LIVED! You must NOW surrender all, trust all, allow all, rest in all. (STAR)

The moment you make the choice to step through this mirror be prepared to be in a constant, conscious state of being presented with life's opportunities to apply the STAR System. At first, you may feel as though you are constantly being tested. There will not seem to be a moment's rest (no pun intended) from your requirement to stay centered in a resting state. Clue: if you are "feeling" tested, you have stepped outside of the mirror and are simply observing it. You've pulled up Mirror Number 4 or 5.   Remember, this mirror is different from the others.   You must enter in.   It is this shift that moves consciousness from "seeking" to "Being."   It takes you to "I AM IS ALL!".

You will be required to **"BE"** the **STAR** as consciousness shifts:

From:	*To:*
I am identity	*I AM identity*
Fear	*Love*
Judgment	*Allowing*
Possessions	*Non Attachment*
Investment in Outcomes	*Divine Order/Plan*
Prejudices	*Preferences*
Personal will	*Divine Will*
Karma	*Grace*

As you are making this shift, remember, so is your Twin. You cannot and do not enter this mirror alone. Two by two they entered the Ark, and two by two you enter the "Arc." The awakened state of awareness within your Twin begins to fuse with the awakened state within you. This is the beginning of reunion. Your Twin does not have to be in your physical proximity for this to take place. You are attuned to each other at the level of Spirit/soul. You are being united, two as One. A new beginning!

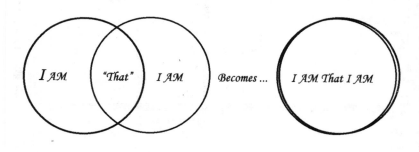

The chart on the following page gives you a composite view of the Seven Sacred Mirrors of Relationships. This chart graphically shows the step by step progression of the mirrors as they open the heart to the wisdom and love revealed through the integration of each mirror.

Seven Sacred Mirrors

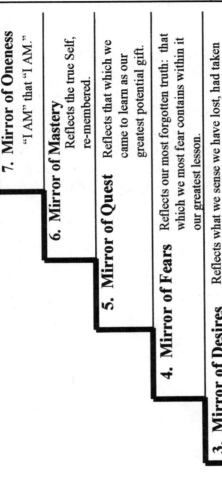

7. Mirror of Oneness "I AM" that "I AM."

6. Mirror of Mastery Reflects the true Self, re-membered.

5. Mirror of Quest Reflects that which we came to learn as our greatest potential gift.

4. Mirror of Fears Reflects our most forgotten truth: that which we most fear contains within it our greatest lesson.

3. Mirror of Desires Reflects what we sense we have lost, had taken away, or never had. That which we most desire reveals our greatest fear.

2. Mirror of Resistance Reflects our charges: that which we resist attracts the opposite of that which we desire.

1. Mirror of Vibration Reflects our magnetic field of attraction: like attracts like, and opposites attract.

Section Four:

The Twin Soul

Relationship

(The Heart of the Matter)

"Lovers don't finally meet somewhere. They're in each other all along."

Jalal-uv-Din Rumi

Opening
New Dimensions
Into Self

Twin Souls are being reunited in great numbers now as the evolution of consciousness approaches the Shift of the Ages so long prophesied by ancient wisdom texts. We are rapidly spiraling into a new dimension of Self understanding and remembered union with all life. An echo of ancient memory is piercing the thin layers of protection that remain around the heart placed there by the alter-ego self. Veils are being lifted. Love is dawning in its fullness as we are being drawn by Love to Love in holy relationship with our God Self. And lo, as Self is revealed, there before the mirrored heart stands our counterpart ... the masculine or feminine aspect of Self ... the beloved Twin that "I AM".

Many of you are now experiencing these new dimensions of Self realization and are thus drawing into your life spiritual relationships of the highest order, including, for some of you, your Twin Soul. You have many questions which the mind naturally presents once the heart has been expanded to experience more of its own mystical Truth. As we approach the subject of Twin Souls and attempt to answer some of these questions, know that the final authority on the subject is you! Your answers will come from your own experience and ultimately from the mystical reunion with your Twin Soul which will take place in alignment with divine Grace. We certainly do not have all the answers, but we are happy to share our understanding which is directly proportional to the level of our own experience.

Questions Most Often Asked About Twin Souls

1. Does everyone have a Twin Soul? If so, how did that come to be?

2. What is the difference between these terms: Twin Soul, Twin Flame and Soulmate?

3. How will I know when I have met my Twin?

4. Is my Twin Soul on earth now? If so, are we destined to meet? Do Twin Souls always recognize each other?

5. Is my Twin Soul necessarily of the opposite gender?

6. Have I always been the same gender in all incarnations?

7. Does each Twin have a soul or is there only one soul? Spirit?

8. Can we communicate with our Twin even though we are not yet together in the flesh? How about if my Twin is not on earth?

9. Does my life affect my Twin Soul and vice versa?

10. Am I subject to the karma of my Twin? Is it the same karma?

11. Do Twin Souls progress in the evolution of consciousness in a parallel fashion?

12. What should I do if I am in a relationship with someone I know is not my Twin? What if I meet my Twin while in another relationship? What do I do then?

13. Once brought together, can Twin Souls ever be in conflict? If so, what causes this? How can conflict be resolved?

14. Once together, can Twin Souls separate or be separated?

15. Are Twin Souls brought together in earth for a specific mission or purpose?

16. What is meant by Twin Soul Reunion? How does this take place?

17. Do Twins move back into the undifferentiated Light following reunion? Do they maintain their individuality?

The Heart of the Matter

1.   Does everyone have a Twin Soul?

Most Definitely! Actually, you could not exist without your Twin Soul because your Twin Soul is the other half of you. It is the masculine or feminine polarity aspect of you that split out of the unified field of Light that you were in the beginning as it lowered itself in frequency in order to experience the materialized world. Thus, we are enabled to participate in the created world and become fully aware and conscious of God's masculine and feminine nature as co-creators in Divine Love. This question requires such an in-depth explanation you may want to return to the section titled: "In the Beginning."

2.   What is the difference between these terms: Twin Soul, Twin Flame and Soulmate?

Twin Soul: Your Self in its opposite polarity. Twin Souls are One in

Spirit and soul and in spiritual origin.

Twin Flame: Same as above...(referencing the Divine Light).

Soulmate: Any other being whose consciousness, mission and purpose is in alignment with yours. In the Absolute, everyone is a potential soulmate.

We use the terms Twin Soul and Twin Flame interchangeably as they have come to be understood by so many to reference the same concept. Some prefer the term Twin Soul for it presents the idea of shared soulship. Others prefer the term Twin Flame because it projects the image of Light from which we emerged. It also reminds the heart of the declaration of great wisdom from the master, Jesus Christ, who referred to each of us as the Light of the world.

3. How will I know when I have met my Twin?

You will not know the answer to this question until you have experienced a mystical reunion with your Twin at some level of Spirit. This could be experienced in the dream state, in deep meditation or through inner knowing at the level of "pure" intuition. Many people now entering into deeply committed and loving relationships believe themselves to be Twin Souls, when in essence they have drawn into their lives a Soulmate who is reflecting their current level of Self knowingness. These are glorious relationships, divine appointments that have been drawn by right of consciousness for the mirroring of deeper oceans of consciousness yet to be revealed to each partner. You will always draw into your life relationships that perfectly reflect your consciousness at the level of your current reality. Twin Soul reunion in the flesh can only occur when there has been a certain degree of union and purification of consciousness with the individual spiritual Self. This individual experience always awakens a high degree of conscious loving ... love of self and love of all. Awakened love with Self releases a high frequency of God Love that becomes the magnetic field of attraction that draws the identical Twin consciousness toward reunion. God is Love. Pure, unconditional, non-judgmental Love. You are Love, your Twin is Love. From Love we came, and unto Love we return. No reunion is possible outside of the consciousness of pure Love.

4.   **Is my Twin Soul on earth now? If so, are we destined to meet? Do Twin Souls always recognize each other?**

Your Twin Soul may or may not be on earth now. In God's house there are many mansion worlds where wisdom, knowledge and learning are acquired. Each of you is on an adventure of learning and may or may not have chosen to incarnate at the same time. We believe there are many factors that enter into the choice for physical incarnation together. It may be determined by a mutual consent as the result of awakening to the individualized Divine Plan of co-creation that would require the combined energies in the flesh to accomplish. For some, earth may be the one mansion world that would provide the energetic environment necessary for Twins to experience the most accelerated awakening.   For others, the particular individual learning experience may be so intense that the other Twin needs to remain in the realms of Spirit in order to hold the Truth for the other without the distractions of the manifest world. In this instance, your Twin would not be here at this time, but you might very well experience inner communications through dreams, meditation or visions.   The determining factor for communication is the vibrational frequency of love that resonates from each Twin Soul in whatever octave they may find themselves to exist. The consciousness of love creates a clear channel for communication from one dimension to another. It is the frequency that empowers us to make conscious contact at the Spirit/soul level.

Twin Souls will always recognize each other to the degree that the veils of the sense of separation from their inner Self have been lifted. The facade body of accumulated memory at the subliminal level of soul may still be so dense for some Twins that recognition would be impossible. It is our belief that if you and your Twin are incarnate together, you will meet up with the other half of yourself at some point. To not do so would defy the laws of consciousness which state that like attracts like. And the more alike, the greater the attraction. You and your Twin will always be the most identical in consciousness of any two souls anywhere. If the love in Self is still somewhat veiled in both Twins, they may enter a very difficult and confusing love/hate relationship that neither can understand. Twins are perfect mirrors for one another and reflect both the Truth and the illusions held in the soul. The intensity of such a relationship becomes so difficult for some that they make the choice not to stay in the relationship.

To conclude the answer to this question, let us emphasize that Twin Souls who have entered into the greatest depth of mastery in love for Self often reference looking into each other's eyes upon their first encounter and feeling something "electric" and extremely "magnetic." There is an inner sense of "coming home" or "looking into the mirror of Self." Often we hear, "I feel like I have known this person forever." They have!

Love is the spiritual glue of consciousness that binds its own to you. To attract YOUR love to you, you must *become* the love that you seek to attract. This is the great *law* of Correspondence! Once Twins are united in

Love, nothing can separate them except their own choice.

5.   Is my Twin Soul necessarily of the opposite gender?

It is important to establish a relationship between the terms "gender" and "polarity." Your Twin will always be the opposite polarity of you. That is, if you are male, you are considered the "positive polarity" of the one soul, and if you are female, you are the "negative polarity" of the one soul. This never changes. The feminine aspect of Self is "negative gender," woman, and the masculine aspect of Self is "positive gender," man. To further answer this we must dive a little deeper into questioning. Look at question number 6.

6.   Have I always been the same gender in all incarnations?

We cannot give you an absolute answer on this question, but we can present some concepts we feel are in alignment with cosmic principles that do not waver. As long as you are in soul alignment with the nature of your polarity, your true Self, your expression of life will always correspond. This is reflective of the law of correspondence which states "like begets like." It is also reflective of the Hermetic principle "as above, so below."

We do believe there are instances where one could possibly incarnate into a body of the opposite gender from the true nature of their divine impulse of polarity. The term for this is a "crossover." As an example, a crossover would be a masculine expression of the one soul incarnated into a female body or vice-versa. But remember, nothing can manifest outside of divine laws. Then how can this occur? To understand this we must embrace the Law of Cause and Effect which states "thoughts held in mind, with deep emotion, manifest after their kind," or after their image and likeness. During the long and arduous experiences of evolution, it can happen that a soul of either polarity becomes so traumatized as a male or female entity that the thought of entering again into an incarnation as another male or female is more than the soul can handle. Within the soul of anyone who has been deeply traumatized there is a continual battle between the divine impulse of the natural forces of life to express and the soul memory of inharmonious, restricted life flow. The male or female soul may then begin to identify with its contra-gender, believing this would be a less painful experience of life, thus choosing a body of the opposite polarity for an incarnation. This is neither good nor bad and must not be judged. It is choice that is made at a soul level in the process of learning and evolving. The only area of concern here is how does this affect the other Twin? This will be addressed in another question.

Another possibility is somewhat opposite in its approach. A fully realized Being, a master of Love who has "consciously" entered into mystical union with the other half of Self, would, by divine law, be capable of incarnating in either a masculine or feminine body. The soul would be in complete harmony with Self, the ONE, and contain the purified consciousness of the ONE LIGHT, masculine and feminine polarity ... the true androgenous state. In order to enter into manifestation, this ONE UNIFIED Soul would need to make a conscious choice and would do so according to the gender that would allow for the greatest opportunity to fulfill the mission or the purpose of that incarnation.

It is important to mention here that the expression of one's sexuality does not directly enter into the concept of twinsoulship. Irrespective of gender or the true nature of individualized polarity, each has free choice in the manner of sexual expression, (either heterosexual or homosexual). Neither expression is exclusively good nor bad. The question does arise, however, to one who has chosen to pursue an intimate relationship of a homosexual nature: "Is this my Twin Soul?" The answer is no, unless the one or both is either a "crossover" or a fully realized Being of Light.

Now, back to the original question: "Have I always been the same gender in all incarnations?" What about those of you who have a vivid past life recall of being the opposite gender from what you are now? Does that mean you have participated in one of the experiences mentioned above? Possibly. But, there are also three other possibilities of which we are aware. One -- you may have a deep subliminal or subconscious desire to be free of all the accumulated painful memories associated with femininity or masculinity. Total recall may be too difficult for you to handle so you may create a vision of seeing yourself as opposite in gender. Two -- it is also possible that, because of the intensity of the karmic ties you have created with others you have encountered in previous incarnations, you may be vicariously recalling an incident through the bonded memories of the other person. Three -- you and your Twin are truly one, and the closer your reunion at the soul level, your past life recall may be that of your contra-gender ... your Twin Soul's memory. You ARE ONE with your other Self, your Twin, and you may be experiencing his or her Soul memory.

7.   Does each Twin have a soul or is there only one soul? Spirit?

Soul is defined as the " entire spectrum of awareness" in each individualized human being. It is an aspect of the "threefold nature of being" of each and every person. Each of us is composed of Spirit, soul and body. The Spirit of God that is contained in your individualized expression of Itself is the same said Spirit contained within every individual. It is the absolute, pure Love nature at the center of every human life. This Spirit expresses itself as One in the Twin Soul, individualized in earth as the masculine and feminine polarity of Itself. At this level of being, the oneness of Twin Souls is known as an eternal reality. Here there is no sense of separation, only the pure expression of the one masculine/feminine Spirit of God.

The soul of each individual is composed of three levels of awareness: conscious, subconscious and Superconscious (or Spirit consciousness). Twin Souls are always conscious of oneness at the level of the Superconscious of soul. The subconscious of each individual functions as a storehouse of memory from both the Superconscious awareness and the conscious awareness of both individualized Twins. It has no volition or discernment capabilities of its own. It simply stores information and makes its impressions of these memories upon the canvas of the conscious mind of each Twin through dreams, visions, thought forms reflective of past perceptions of experiences, or thought forms lowered in light frequency as divine ideas from the Superconscious or Spirit. Twin Souls, in essence, share these two levels of consciousness, but perceive these levels in differing degrees of awareness. At the level of the One Spirit, the essence of Being is shared as pure Love, pure wisdom, pure knowingness. To the degree that each is aware of that level will it be known. At the level of subconscious and conscious soul memory, their awareness is directly proportional to the depth of total recall of the vast accumulated memories of each Twin's experiences stored within the one subconscious that is shared by both. Without full recall, each Twin may experience feelings and emotions that are the effects of the thought forms impressed upon the sensitive plate of the subconscious level of awareness that is shared by both. Often this is perceived as sudden inner joy and happiness or sudden explosions of sadness, depression, fear, etc., that neither can logically explain. This we call the shared contra-gender memories of consciousness at the soul level of the subconscious.

So, just as the Twins are one in Spirit, they are one in soul. Remember, soul is the entire spectrum of awareness. That includes conscious, subconscious and Superconscious (Spirit). They share one soul, but they may not be aware of doing so until each Twin moves through the depth of the subconscious memories. Carl Jung said the purpose of existence is to make the subconscious conscious. We take that a step further and say our purpose is to make both the subconscious and the Superconscious conscious, for herein lies the experience of pure ONEness with all aspects of the levels of awareness in their purest states. Once all channels of consciousness are open, we receive pure information and have pure experience. This creates an environment in consciousness, a magnetic field of attraction, that draws us into ascension and reunion of twinsoulship as the known eternal reality of the One being -- masculine, feminine God Self.

8.   Do we communicate with our Twin even though we are not yet together in the flesh? What if my Twin is not on earth?

Now that we have an understanding of the oneness shared by Twin Souls at the Spirit/soul level, we can grasp a deeper awareness of how communications can transpire between them. To the degree that each Twin is in alignment with and open to Spirit/soul will that communication be made possible. If there is a vast amount of false beliefs, error perceptions or fears still occupying space in their linked subconscious memories, communications will be difficult at the level of purity and clarity that is desired. It behooves each Twin, then, to be ever desiring the experience of mystical union with his or her indwelling Spirit. It is also a top priority to be willing to release any false ideas that have accumulated in each soul. This is accomplished with the purest heart's yearning to know God and a daily dedicated willingness to surrender to the baptism of fire in the soul by the regenerative power of the Holy Spirit. It is also important to note here that any pure heart intention to make contact with your Twin Soul is immediately received at the level of Spirit of the other. So, speak to your beloved through your shared heart. Hold them in the acknowledgment of their freedom in the soul. Embrace them with a magnetic love vibration released through the conscious extension of regenerative thoughts such as, "I love you ... I support you ... I believe in you. I am here for you. We are one!" It makes no difference whether your Twin Soul is incarnate or not.

Communication between Twins is always at the Spirit/soul level. Even if your Twin is on earth now, and you are drawn together in the flesh, your deepest communications will occur on inner levels. Such is the glory and blessing of oneness. If your Twin is on earth, and you have not drawn together yet, the greater the intensity of the love vibration that is released in every conscious thought, the greater the magnetic attraction for your Twin.

9. Does my life affect my Twin Soul and vice versa?

Yes! Think about it. If you and your Twin Soul are one ... and you most certainly are, how could your life not affect your Twin? Every thought, feeling, deep emotion, experience, action, prayer, stored memory, overcoming, and revelation has an effect. You cannot do unto yourself that you do not do unto your other self. What a glorious revelation this becomes to everyone who awakens to this great cosmic truth. Not only are you living your life for yourself, you are living your life for another you ... the polarized opposite half of you expressing somewhere, in some time or no time, as the case may be. What you do for one, you do for two in One. In the realest sense possible, you are your Beloved's keeper.

Because most incarnated souls are not completely free of fragmented realities, however, that which is thought, felt, or experienced by one Twin is not necessarily received by the other as a knowing of the actual experience. It is transmitted as an energy frequency of intensity directly proportional to the emotion or feeling of the thought, action or experience of the transmitter. It is usually received by the other Twin as an unrelated emotion to what they may be currently experiencing or thinking.   For example, one Twin may have accomplished something really magnificent. Something he or she has been pursuing for a long time. The other Twin may be just having an ordinary day, and all of a sudden he or she is filled with great joy for no apparent reason. The opposite effect can also happen. One Twin may wake up one morning full of joy and anticipation about something, and all of a sudden, because their other Self becomes very depressed about something, that emotion may be transferred to the Twin that was in joy.   And, back and forth these deeply felt emotions swing. This can result in great confusion and a sense of being scattered for no reason, or the opposite -- feeling peace and joy that passes the understanding of one's current reality check.

The depth of this Truth can be the most empowering knowledge for transformation, for it helps you relinquish the reasoning mind to the need for discernment of all the feelings and emotions that are experienced by you in any given day. It inspires you to know the Truth at all times for yourself and your Beloved. Regardless of what you may be feeling in your personal life, the awareness of any negative emotion or false belief is a STAR signal to enter into your Spirit in surrender, trust, allowing and rest. This is a true response from the level of I AM that will always activate the only true emotion, LOVE! You and your Beloved will simultaneously be transformed and lifted immediately.

10.   Am I subject to the karma of my Twin? Is it the same karma?

Ah, this is a good one! And, you may not like the answer, but we will offer it to you anyway. The term "karma" has become so user friendly that it is even found in Webster's Dictionary. It is defined by Webster as: "the force generated by a person's actions that determines his destiny in his next existence." If we take this definition seriously, we are doomed indeed! So, let us dispel the myth of karma right up front. Nothing determines your destiny except your current level of consciousness as it rests, either in or out of alignment with the Divine Plan of the nature of LOVE that is written in your heart. We suggest you read that sentence several times.

The reason so many people "think" they are living their current life as one reaping the harvest of karmic debt is because they simply continue to make the same old choices in consciousness they have made lifetime, after lifetime, after lifetime. They are still caught up in the threadless spin of consciousness patterned in alignment with the past. Over and over they choose to pass judgment. Again and again they will not allow themselves to risk loving unconditionally. They continually evade looking at their deepest fears, and pattern themselves in behaviors that protect them from the removal of the masks and veils of conscious and subconscious illusions. The alter-ego continues to sit on the throne of consciousness making the same choices, decisions, and demands of control that were made throughout eons of previous incarnations. Round and round they go. Where they stop ... only they can know!

To the degree that each Twin makes moment by moment choices in its soul, which are in direct alignment with the true nature of reality in Spirit, will they no longer be subject to the merry-go-round of the karmic debt accumulated as their or their Twin's repetitive choices. Remember, Twins are one at the level of Spirit and "soul!" Once each individualized polarity of consciousness chooses pure LOVE ideas, expressions and emotions, they then become subject to each other's GRACE, and this becomes their newly shared karma. AH!

11. Do Twin Souls progress in the evolution of consciousness in a parallel fashion?

Yes! This is a truth of great importance, and complies with the Master's teaching of the degree of unity with all human beings. He emphasized the fact that if He was lifted in consciousness, it would in turn lift others to His state. This is especially true for Twin Souls because of the identical resonance field that vibrates between them either in or out of manifestation. Twin Souls progress much like your right and left feet progress as they cover a given mile. One moves forward in the process of the journey which automatically provides the impetus to bring the other forward in similar fashion. Then as the progression would have it, the one that was previously the hind foot becomes the leading one. They alternate in a rhythmic sequence of harmony and balance unfolding, growing, stretching, exploring together in the yin/yang of conscious evolution. As each polarized expression of God's energy becomes fully balanced and complete in awareness, this assists the balancing and completion of awareness in the contra-gender of the other.

12. What should I do if I am in a relationship with someone I know is not my Twin? What if I meet my Twin while in another relationship? What do I do then?

Whatever relationship you are in at this moment is perfect for you. It is serving you as your greatest opportunity to become a fully awakened master of LOVE! Whoever is in your life is there as a divine appointment in perfect resonance with your consciousness on all levels. Remember, "life is consciousness." This great cosmic law will not be mocked. But you say, "I don't get along with this person. He/She is completely different from me. We have nothing in common. I know this relationship is a 'karmic' one only." Oh, really? Now, what have you learned about karma? What do you know about consciousness? No one can be in your life that is not a mirrored reflection of a state of consciousness, *on some level*, that is resonating in alignment with your own. To completely understand this great truth, you must fully comprehend the mystical principles embraced in the 7 Sacred Mirrors of Relationships.

If you are seriously making a decision to leave any current relationship that has become more than an acquaintance, we strongly encourage you to do so only at the purest heart level of love. That means that you leave with no ill feelings in your heart. That means you make your decision, not out of strong prejudice or judgment of the other's behavior, but out of compassion, love and total acceptance of the other in their choices for their experience of life. That means that in the deepest recesses of your heart you desire the highest and best for the other person. There can be no exceptions here, for to leave backpacking in anything less than unconditional love will only delay the reunion with your Twin Soul. Twin Souls only unite in *pure unconditional love* as *pure unconditional love*! We cannot emphasize this enough.

Please don't hear us say it is not O.K. to make changes in relationships. Often, people will come together to share the depth of consciousness in each other as a spiritual gift toward the empowerment of eternal life. Once that gift has been received, it very well may be time to move on to accept the next gift. It is just as unhealthy to stay in a relationship that has completed its divine appointment as it is to leave a relationship that is not complete. Only *your* heart will tell you when a relationship is complete.

We often hear of Twin Souls finding each other while still involved in another relationship. Again, we emphasize that to leave without spiritual closure is to sentence yourself "guilty" with just cause. You will serve your time, and, even if you have met your Twin, the fire of that relationship will be so hot because of the identical mirrored reflection that you will more than likely not be able to withstand the pressure.

At the same time, remember that Twins grow in consciousness parallel with one another, progressing very rapidly. If you are not in relationship with your Twin, you are in a relationship with the Twin of someone else. Their twinsoulship is progressing at the level of their combined consciousness. You may have stretched beyond your capacity to remain in the old relationship, especially if your partner is unable to stretch with you. Sometimes, to stay would be to stagnate each other and not be for the highest good. Only your heart will know. Never leave a relationship because the grass looks greener. Leave only because you know the harvest is complete within the field that you have sown together.

13. Once brought together, can Twin Souls ever be in conflict? If so, what causes this? How can conflict be resolved?

The answer to the first part of this question is most definitely, YES! As a matter of fact, we do not know any Twin Soul couple who has not been faced with what we call the final initiation or firewalk of the soul. Any relationship of a lesser degree than twinsoulship could not withstand the intensity of the battle the alter-ego initiates in its final struggle for a stronghold in consciousness. What causes this conflict? The mirrors of soul. You are standing before your naked self, and the cellulite of consciousness can find no place to hide. Nothing can remain hidden or camouflaged in the presence of the pure Light that you are. Any shadows that seek to hide behind the Son will be drawn forth by the Light. The game plays of the alter-ego can no longer withstand the pressures of the Master Mind that sees through them. Gazing into the eyes of your

Beloved, the fire of your love for and in each other penetrates to the volcanic core of consciousness. You will not be able to discern whose shadow is surfacing, for there is only one shadow between you. You have become the manifestation of each other's dreams, realities and illusions. You will not be allowed to have any other gods before you except I AM *that* I AM.

There is an integration of soul and Spirit that takes place in Twin Soul Reunion that can be likened to an alchemical change that can only be experienced rather than understood or grasped with the mind. It is a blending of all the ingredients of heart and mind that compose the completed matrix of Self realized which must embrace both polarities of positive and negative energies expressing union and harmony at the conscious, subconscious and Superconscious levels of soul. Each Twin has grown in wisdom and learning from his or her own individualized polarity of experience. Their opposite or contra-gender awareness has come through the experiences of their other Self as emotions and feelings that do not equate with their own experiences. Having lived in the sense of separation for so long, it is difficult to allow integration to become the balancing factor without resistance from the alter-ego. This can create confusion for the soul that has seen itself as separate from its counterpart in the process of countless evolutions.

To help clarify this idea lets take a look at the maturity of the soul quality "strength" for instance. The male, or positive expression of the one consciousness, has experienced strength as the expression of bold ideas, taking charge, being in control -- mentally, physically and emotionally. The female or negative expression of the one consciousness has experienced "strength" as non-resistance, patience, quiet endurance, etc. The wisdom and love gleaned by both entities must now be integrated to become the complete expression of "strength." This integration takes place without any conflict only if there is no conflict left in the soul of each one to be alchemied. There will always be conflict to the degree that there are any differences of perceptions anchored in judgment, feelings and emotions that have not fully embraced the contra-gender experience or that have not been resolved within Self.

One of the most powerful tools for conflict resolution that we have embraced is calling forth assistance from ascended beings of Light who are always there in their fully Christed state of consciousness ready to embrace you both in the transformative vibration of unconditional love. The governing law of this planet, however, is free will, and they will not impose their assistance without an invitation. It is always true: the more love gathered together in focused intention, the more powerful and swift the healing.

Finally, all of consciousness must be surrendered to Divine Will. This allows for the movement of Spirit to infuse its Divine Light at the highest intensity. A healing will take place, but we have observed that the way of the healing often surpasses any mental perception we might have as to "how" the resolution will come to pass. Almost invariably, something is revealed through each encounter that was deeply camouflaged by an old defensive behavior pattern. Had the conflict not arisen, the patterned control mechanism would not have been triggered.

Resolution, then, can be as simple as one, two, three: (1) intend the heart to desiring above all else the return to harmony; (2) ask for assistance; and (3) surrender to Divine Will. For a deeper understanding as to the cause of conflict in all relationships, review the section on the 7 Sacred Mirrors of Relationships.

14. Once together, can Twin Souls separate or be separated?

Nothing can separate Twin Souls. They are one soul forever. They are the union of the Divine in It's Divine Idea of Itself. Their eternal union is at the Spirit and Superconscious level of Being. In the manifest state, Twins experience a sense of separation, but only at the level of soul that is still hidden from the Light of Love they truly are. Their individual awakening to the eternal love nature within their polarized expression of the One is the catalyst that activates remembered union at the soul level. Fully awakened at all levels of soul, they can never be separated in consciousness again. Expressing individualized polarized Self at the manifest level of existence, however, always allows for free will choice as to whether Twin Souls will remain together in the close proximity of relationship. Depending on the commitment to walk through the fire, to honor the mirroring of self, to heal and stay conscious at all costs, these factors will influence that free will choice. So, yes, Twin Souls can separate once brought together in the earth, but more than likely the level of love that has been remembered within each Twin in order to draw them together is more than sufficient to provide the magnetic field that empowers them to stay together. And, not only stay together, but accomplish a great work for humanity.

15. Are Twin Souls brought together in earth for a specific mission or purpose?

The answer to this question is yes, but the reasoning behind this answer usually eludes even the Twins. It is not that the Twins have been united for a "specific" mission or purpose, but that their fully realized state of consciousness opens them to the creative flow of Spirit which always seeks to "serve" in love, beauty, joy and creativity. Their union of forces also multiplies and empowers them, far beyond the power of two individuals. It multiplies the power of ONE which contains within it unlimited, boundless, infinite numbers of creative potential. A master of love always finds fulfillment in service of some kind, either to humankind specifically or to the beauty and betterment of life in general. Twin Soul Reunion is Love united, and it is the nature of LOVE to serve. Service is the mission and plan written at the center of all Beings created in the image and likeness of God. Service to others and life becomes the driving force within Twin Souls, and according to the divine selection of each Twin Soul Unit will that service manifest.

In examining the lives of all the Twin Souls we know, and the Twins of recorded history, each unit of One has, and is, contributing wonderful gifts that are changing or have changed the course of humankind. We also find, in interviewing Twin Soul couples, that they were engaged in service of some kind long before the meeting of the Twin. Either that, or they were in the midst of a career shift moving toward that service at the time of their meeting. Service becomes their passion and their love. It is a glorious thing to witness the working together of a Twin Soul unit. They are empowered to accomplish great things and influence the direction of human evolution within the Divine Plan.

16.   What is meant by Twin Soul Reunion? How does that take place?

Twin Soul Reunion is fusion that takes place within the consciousness of both Twins as their masculine and feminine polarities of consciousness are harmoniously blended to become the One Known. Our experience has been that this takes place gradually through the process of transformation, regeneration, infusion and defusion on all levels of consciousness within each Twin. When a certain vibrational frequency of love becomes the sustaining magnetic field of consciousness, then the Twins may have what is described as a cosmic experience of union with their individualization of I AM and their shared I AM. This experience has been reported as an individual one, unique to each Twin, or as an experience that took place within them simultaneously. It is a celestial Nova event that is beyond measure, explanation and words to describe. In the final union, that state of unified consciousness becomes the forever state of knowing that is shared between the two, whether in or out of time. It becomes the eternal life consciousness of the two in the One. The sense of separation is forever gone. They share a fully awakened consciousness at the level of Spirit, soul and body.

How does this take place? God only knows. And, when will this take place? God only knows. Cosmic union is most assuredly governed by God I AM. It is a matter of divine timing that takes place when there is a readiness of consciousness within each soul. There is no measure of persuasion or influence, no begging, bargaining or pleading that will force the Creator to make this fusion. It is part of the glorious mystery that will forever be. We do know that Love is the magnetic field of attraction that speeds the propulsion of consciousness to make it ready, but we also are very clear that the precise moment is a Godly choice. It is the ultimate gift of Grace.

17. Do Twins move back into the undifferentiated Light following reunion? Do they maintain their individuality?

We believe reunion takes place in an upward progressive fashion through the expansion of consciousness in this manner. First, there is the reunion with the individual I AM Self of each person. Consciousness thus expanded in awareness of oneness with individual Self automatically is drawn into the greater expanded consciousness of the reunion of Self in the opposite polarity, or Twin Soul. As absolute fusion is experienced at the Twin Soul level and by the nature of the cosmic unity of ALL Life, an expansion again takes place as the Twin Soul Unit begins to experience union with others of similar vibrations of love resonance. This is experienced as inner *knowingness* of oneness on an even grander scale than oneness with Self and Twin. This would ultimately result in the reunification in consciousness of the oneness of all people. This, of course, would not be the ultimate unification either. There are many mansions, and many created Beings in those many mansions of God's House or Kingdom. Just because they are not visible to us does not in any way deny their existence. Union of consciousness at the global level would then facilitate the ushering in of evolution into union at the cosmic level. The nature of God and God's creations is infinite, and the stages of union must also be infinite.

When we speak of moving back into the undifferentiated Light, we are talking about undifferentiated Light as consciousness that knows only expression in oneness. In the beginning we were all "THE" undifferentiated Light without divine selective individualization or expression. In other words, we were pure consciousness, but not conscious of being conscious. The process of the Soular Reunion is one of ever expanding levels of becoming conscious of being conscious or conscious of Consciousness in full and unlimited expression. So, the answer to the first part of this question is, "Yes, we move back into the undifferentiated Light of Consciousness, fully conscious of oneness with the Light and with all! Thus, we become fully Real -'I'-zed, conscious co-creators 'of' God!"

Do we maintain our individuality? Yes and No! We must understand that once reunion of polarized consciousness is experienced as a constant, we will be in such a different state of awareness that our current grasp of *who* and *what* we *are* will be altered dramatically from our present understanding. Our individuality will be fully united with *our other* individuality. Therefore, we will be conscious of both aspects of our Self united as ONE knowingness composed of the unlimited consciousness of positive and negative undifferentiated Light. In other words, our concept of "individuality" will embrace the two as ONE. We would also, then, be fully capable of making the choice of manifesting a body as "either" polarity of the One, or we could choose to enter manifestation in any dimension as masculine and feminine expressions of the One Being of Light. To try to perceive our future unlimited and boundless potential with our present limited, finite consciousness is impossible. This is de-ja-vu in reverse and cannot be done. But, we can allow our hearts to overflow with rivers of joy as we open in great anticipation to our infinite divine potential.

Section Five:

The Soular Reunion

"When you make the two one, and when you make the inside like the outside and the outside like the inside, and the above as the below, and when you make the male and the female one and the same, ... then shall you enter the Kingodm."

The Gospel of Thomas 22

Look not to find yourself
within yourself anymore.
But seek to find your other half,
beckoning you to
penetrate through and embrace.
The one which is looking is the one looking
at that to which it seeks to know in
I Am of the other One!
Such we begin in the journey home to find
the Self now in the other.
Not in the Self as before,
for that door has opened wide.
If you would help and seek the other
Self of you in the other One,
then you will understand
the fragments that seem to be in you.

DiadrAna 6/2/96
"And the Master Said"

The Reunion:

Your minds are in a powerful place now to begin the ascension of the Soular Reunion. As your heart rests in open acceptance of the All, this environment creates a metamorphosis as it does in the butterfly as its cocoon is opening. Rest assured that which is to be given freedom was implanted in the Soul of the One which you are ... in the beginning. The Soular Reunion marks a new journey, a new beginning into the heavens while still in the earth. It is a rising and a transmutation of that which is given in the earth for a time. The Master, Beloved, has risen. So it is with you.

And as you expand the idea of you, you shall know the oneness of it all. So with the reunion unto the cosmic I AM with the All in All. It is the cosmic union of the beloved Son returned in earth. Multiplied a thousand times, that which you know now shall be revealed in time. The key is to "let" it be revealed and not to force the knowing to come. As you sit with the love of One in the other One, it shall be given for you to know. The Master Teacher is with you in all ways. You are that Master in one idea of Self.

The essence of God's nature within you is so completely inclusive that your evolution within that nature will ultimately embrace the total conscious recall of the Word within the Word. Worlds within worlds will begin to unfold into your mirrored vision, and you will be drawn into each one through the eternal spiral of consciousness inward. Union with Self, begets union with Other Self. Union with Other Self begets union with Global Self. Union with Global Self begets union with Cosmic Self. Union with Cosmic Self begets union with Infinite Self.

And there is probably much more, but the finite mind can not grasp the Infinite, much less beyond that.

The soul is "boundless," and to experience that boundlessness consciousness begins an ever expanding embrace of the One in all. You will find in the Soular Reunion a growing number of souls that are attracted into your life with which there is a harmonic resonance of purity and awakened Divinity as never before. You will begin to feel "family all are we," and, like the Master Teacher, you will call them intimate "friends." You will begin to feel as though you have known many of those who come to share in your gatherings of Light. "Have we ever met before?" becomes the salutation of first time meetings. Perhaps, perhaps not. What is happening is your magnetic field of attraction is becoming part of a "collective" clustering of souls of similar vibrational frequency. Love is awakening Love in all, and within its tender embrace "re-members" its Self. As these gatherings continue to multiply in service and in prayer, the whole becomes greater than the sum of its parts. Consciousness approaches a new Omega Point.

This is the "Single Eye" consciousness of the ancient wisdom texts that transcends polarity while living in polarity. From this viewpoint it has microscopic and macroscopic vision and can see the within of all things, and the unity thereof.

For the past two years, the inner Spirit continues to emphasize the two by two journey that is now reaching cosmic proportions. We are assured over and over we do not go on from here alone. We are entering the era of the Bodhisattva. We are also being told that assistance is given to those who ask for it by Beings of pure Light who live within the inner worlds simply awaiting the opening of our seals to establish communication links. It is not by chance we are simultaneously entering a "communications" era empowering us to "link-up" through global web sites of infinite numbers. Never before have we had access to so much knowledge or to instant communication with each other. This is not by chance. It is all the outer reflection of the inner consciousness which is opening to more of itself. We are reuniting with the One!

We really have no idea where we are going except "Home." We are homeward bound in our boundless state. The kingdom of God is beckoning our exploration and experience. The many mansions of worlds within worlds is becoming our playground, and we, created in the image and likeness of God, are becoming free to vacation wherever we will and partake of the eternal Tree of Life. It is a glorious journey.

"*Two by two
they entered the ark,
now two by two
they enter the arc.*"
We are One!

We felt guided to include in this section readings received from our Twin Soul Spirit, which are relative to the Soular Reunion and twinsoulship. These messages came at various times over a period of about 2 years in our prayer sessions. In some of the messages, we are addressed by our spiritual names, Diadra and Ana. When being referred to as the Twin Soul unit, Spirit calls us by the name DiadrAna (a composite of the two in one). I liked my Spiritual name and had it changed when John and I were married. John still prefers to be called, John.

Some of the teachings are addressed specifically to us, but most of them are teachings for the masses. We share them as a collective for they are all relevant to the subject of twinsoulship for everyone. The messages were tape recorded and then transcribed word for word by our dear friend Pat whose love, support and tireless service continue to bless us. We hope these words bless you as they have us, and that the wisdom and love expressed comforts your heart as you remember, re-member who you are.

Blessings,

DiadrAna

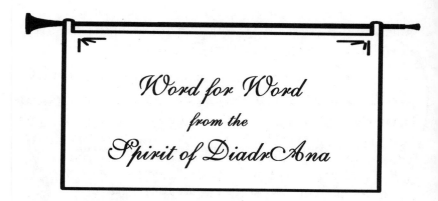

Word for Word
from the
Spirit of Diadr Ana

*T*his time of separation for the two of you is for the quickening of the flame of the units of two in the One. Love generated to a certain frequency of intensification brings forth a new birth and a new creation, Genesis Two.

Trust that the energy you feel in the separation is a quickening agent for co-creation and not one of fear, but one of longing for the new life that it is giving birth through the intensity of the separated state. As you long to be in the presence of one another, this kindles the fire in the heart to an intensified vibratory frequency necessary to move that energy in the environmental situations and bring you into situations in which your energy can be experienced in proximity. Each of you will experience different energy intensifications and movements during this time frame of reference.

Sit often, both of you, during this time of separation with corresponding thoughts of remembrance. These are attracting forces which unite, in the flesh, that which is in the soul and the Spirit.

This is the Omega and the Alpha, an unusual time of combined energy forces spiraling in opposite directions pulling an end to a beginning and a beginning to an end. *3/30/94*

*M*ystical union in a man and woman does not take place as supposed. It flows like a current in a stream. There is no coming together, for it is already that which you seek. The heart opens to remember that which is true already in space. The love to which I AM in you now knows its own and forever reviews itself as I AM One. If you will allow this energy to penetrate into that which has forgotten, the day shall come in the earth that all of you that is I AM shall remember it to be true of you as One. *5/2/96*

*T*he love that grows between you is like the flower that blooms in the earth in the spring. Having gone through the death of winter, it has forgotten its beauty. But as the sun draws it forth, it remembers the Life Force upon which it lives and in which it lives. It is whole and complete within itself. Treasures are being poured within this relationship. . . gifts of Love and Grace that are too numerous to be mentioned. It is that which has been written within you for eons of time, since the very beginning. As you hold one another in each other's heart, know that this is that which draws you together. Remembered love always draws unto itself that which is remembered. Rest in each other's hearts during this time of separation until the time of the flesh when you can rest in each other's arms. The angels of love surround you both and flutter to the heart's surface the remembrance of your resting in the Spirit together. Every time you remember one another, you draw together more in the earth. Hold each one in love's embrace, releasing, releasing, releasing. Hold each other in love's embrace as one eternal flame united in the freedom of the love that resonates between you. 4/19/94

It is written in the heart of I AM, Twin Flames of love emerged in the beginning from the flame of God's heart centered in the core of all or Om. Compulsed by love to move forward into existence, you propelled and propelled and propelled until the impulse at the center of love caused a split in the flame, bursting forth the Life Force in each of you as I AM, beginning again, going forth. It is written now that you come together united again by the flame in the flame I AM. Corresponding experiences unite you as each individualization of the One becoming two has divided, multiplied and increased, knowing itself as I AM again. Moved upon the waters and the face of the earth, it became a living being of eternal life, immersed in the seas, written in the wind, carried in the life, moving in the stars. It is written I AM Om. Carrying forth the Life Force, it moved upon the face of the waters, into the seas of the deep, emerging into the land becoming I AM Om. Having encountered one another in the way of the One, Christ now encouraged the Life Force to begin to expand Itself, splitting in the flame of the heart, moving the One into the two. Two by two they entered the ark.

Purity of the Life Force enabled new life to begin within the center core of the split of the flame of the I AM. Precious moments in the earth enabled the Life to continue to expand bringing more of Itself into being. Entering time and time again, the Life Force quickened in each, in each, in each, moving, moving, moving, carrying forth Itself into love. Encounters in the earth are not easy, for they tend to drain the Life Force of Itself. In the tendency to be drained, the faith is quickened, and it increases the One in the many. Living Itself in the flame of love, the flame of Light ignites and moves the One into the Being of the Light.

Almighty I AM returning home once again, bringing into the earth a new dimension and a new beginning for all the children of the earth to see. The quickening heart flame ignites, ignites, assisted by the love lights of those who go beyond. Penetrating into the earth field, the magnetic pull draws, inward, inward, inward, moving inward, two becoming One, two becoming One, spiraling, spiraling, spiraling.

Excursions into dimensions of Father/Mother God's createdness have brought your individual consciousness to a place of recognition and absorption in the love that recognizes itself in I AM in you. Each time you have been expelled into I AM temples of love in many other dimensions, the capacity for growing in awareness has increased.

There have been a multitude of experiences that have fallen short of the Divine Plan written in the heart of DiadrAna. These experiences resulted in what you now are experiencing as "healing of your internal soul" through the quickening of the fire of love which is bringing you both into remembrance of that which I AM. Each time you come together in the earth at the present moment of time, this will intensify the remembering of lost lives, as well as those which were united. Pain separates the soul in itself as far as it believes it to be One or not One.
5/18/94

*Y*ou must understand that the painful experiences brought about by karma, as you understand it, or those events that have not been in alignment with the Divine Plan written in DiadrAna, accumulated in memory and brought forth pain and suffering according to human separateness and the belief in separation. Catalytic events also influenced this belief system, which resulted in the sense of separateness. Accumulated catalytic, as well as free will choices of separateness, resulted in the remembrances of scars in the soul that are now being healed.

Each one of you has served in the earth in several capacities, both together and apart. Each one of you has had, at the center core of all impulse learning, the Divine Plan that quickens the soul aspect of the nature of the children of God... that which needed to be remembered in order to be expressed as a fully realized child of God.

Let us be assured, beloved ones, the drawing together of your hearts was in the control of the Divine Union Plan written there as one seed of love. Compelled by this love, you came together, loving one another even as the Master had taught. Beyond all man made laws and human conditions in the moment, the love could not be contained. Unicircle flames of the One which spiral between you in the eternal life circle must be expressed when encountered in earth life.

It is written in the children of God the units of oneness that reside. Energy patterns are now being attracted to one another according to the vibratory frequency of the past in alignment with the current circle of light that now moves according to the individual choices made at the heart's core. It is the path that returns the love of God back into the image of Itself, remembering I AM that I AM, reflecting I AM that I AM.

Rest in the softness of your hearts, allowing the other to rest at the same moment in time within you. Gather one upon the other, gather one into the other. Merge, merge, merge. Mind merges, heart merges, soul merges, body merges, united, united, united. Centered, centered, each occupying one space, one time, one memory, one being, one presence, one power, one work, one life.

The love that measures itself between you as One calls you to the measure of Itself. It is not to be understood, but it is to be that experience of One. As you unite in love, that which you thought you had remembered will soon be left to itself, and that which remembers you will be taken into the heart for eternal life.

It is written I AM. We are Om. DiadrAna moves in the earth, drawing forth Itself among the many. Time is coming to pass united in love we stand, One, One, One -- embraced by the light of I AM in each one of you. You'll reflect only that which is reflected, that which I AM is. God's love reflects I AM in the image of all. See only this vision as you look into the eyes of each child of God. Stand together, gazing into the I AM image that you see in one another, for I AM there, and I unite you in Myself as well as in each other. Union in One and union in each becomes union in God in the earth, bringing forth new life, new birth, new gifts of love.

Thus, you glorify Me with a glory I had with Thee in the beginning of I AM. Mission completes as you move forward in the earth united, united, in love. Love is I AM circled flame of light. In the beginning, One, One, One, One.

5/18/94

As the energy systems of both of you are entwined in the One, there is a balancing factor moving into place. All shifts of energy which seem to take you out of the circle of love are that which is scattered in the heart to assimilate and find its resonance with that which is eternal in the One. The Light is bringing all to the surface of the one unit of love in measured time. Hold that which is dear in your heart, each other. Let not any fragments of earth's dust cloud that vision. Return, return, return into the DiadrAna. Do not return into that which is not of that which I AM. The collective memory of the DiadrAna is awakening. Scattered collectives gather in the One as that which belongs to that which you are comes to remember that which is I AM. You are *that* only.   *6/1/95*

*R*ainbow colors are not separate. One merges into the other, lending its hue. Soft. No conflict here. Such is my promise for peace. Give each other that which you need. Master teacher emerging. Difficult as two polar opposites unite. Extremes meet. Gentleness and strength. Christ abides. Collect. You are not joined as two ends tied together in a knot. You are joined as two spectrums merging, from one extreme to another ... Light, and variations of that Light form, uniting. Give each other what you need. Night follows day, day follows night. Polar opposites of extreme light and darkness come together at sunset and sunrise without conflict. *4/30/95*

*C*oming together in time you are DiadrAna, the one unit of Holy Light gathering its own idea. All the spaces that you have occupied, the multitudes of faces presented into the realms, now come together as One. The coming together is a combination, a coronation, and a collection of all that which you truly are. And so the masks of time worn in spaces beyond and here fall away. Thus you feel scattered days and energies not compatible to what the normality of all to which you wore in the past would hold. Seek not to be of the past. Measure it not. And so allow that which is in you to fulfill its own idea by resting where it will. Moving fast and still. Let it be. Trust.
12/12/95

*H*onor differences, for there will be differences. Even in your relationship, there will be differences. It is imperative for differences to come together in union to complement one another, to make the fullness of the rose expressed.

God is not of sameness ever. Even the snow flakes are different. Difference is one of the greatest honors you can bestow upon one another as you honor the differences, honor, honor.

It is important that as you enter into this relationship you honor the needs of one another as you cope with the energy in Terra. And each of you will have somewhat different needs, although some will be identical. Each one of you has developed coping mechanisms for the energy in Terra. Honor these coping mechanisms. Do not try to change one another. Honor one another. This will become a teaching of the Twin Souls, the Twin Souls, the Twin Souls. It is imperative that Twin Souls learn the great gift of Grace incorporated in honor.
7/25/94

*F*ocus many hours in prayer now. It is important. Each one of you. For in this still silence, together you come. My energy is more than One. I penetrate through the veils of time, communicating with you. And every time the heart intends itself to willed ideas of our God, the gates of hope fly open wide. And so it is the Kingdom's energy patterns moving to welcome you in. So be it.

Believe, trusting now that which you are given each day to encounter so that it comes for you to be a blessing and a measuring unit for love's obeying. Seek only to serve the love which you know to be in Truth. Loving one another, your mission unfolds, as do others. Many, many, many coming into this idea. *12/12/95*

At the point of light within the mind of God,
I Am.
At the point of love within the heart of God,
I Am.
I Am the way, the truth, the life.
My way is the way.
The link, the link, the link.
At the point of light within the heart of God,
I Am.
At the point of love within the heart of God,
I Am.   7/27/94

The power of our love
is not as it appears to be,
but far beyond what the eye can see.
And now impulsed by the heart of God,
we are being returned.

Journey homeward.
Hallowed ground. Believe!.
And as you come into my arms,
you do not come alone.
Two by two I bring you home.

United in my holy love,
impulsed by the heavenly dove,
the spirit of my light and love
the winged one within your heart,
is One, not two apart!

Open your eyes.
Let not your heart entertain any doubt
ever, ever, ever, again!
This is the only remaining sin,
the doubt that still lives within.

Offer this as your gift of love
and let my eternal heavenly dove
bring it a new beginning,
and spiral it into a spin
so that only Truth remains within.   *12/3/94*

In the beginning was the Word, and the Word was love. And love begot itself as DiadrAna, Light of the world. Opening Itself to that which It is, It separated to become more of that recognized eye to eye within Itself. Thus is the beginning. And now in the beginning of that which has begot, that which has begun shall begin again. Not a new beginning, so to speak, from an old one, never to be remembered, but a beginning that is revealed into Itself again, standing forth into the Light, seeing that which is I AM Om Aum. And here we have a new beginning in the beginning. You are a fragmentation yet to. be revealed of all the totality of that which you are. *4/11/95*

Together
all the lights will gather in the One
and glorify the Only Begotten Son.
And thus we stand before our Lord,
fully unionized in time,
giving life and life again.
Such is the Divine Plan.
Omni Ashni Aum
I Am!

Moving in time, the light carries forth that which is given. Continue now to believe in that which you I AM are. We are one light of love. Together we become that which is written in OUR heart ... One. Oh, DiadrAna, the will and work of the Master herein resides within the cellular structure of the feminine and the masculine energy forms in which you find yourselves to be. This is a given in time, a unit of One. 4/12/95

Light is a beginning. There are photons of light everywhere, and as each light wave unit moves in assignment, that which is written emerges. At this particular time in space, all light photons are coming together to express one-ness. And thus we have what is considered in time and understood in mastery to be what is referred to as "a new beginning in time/space" for all photon light wave beings. You are One. And as this Light explodes in time, thus all is affected and returns to Itself. Loving one another now, move forward in this new beginning. Allowing is the secret of all time. Do not force. Do not resist. Do not try to understand. Allow is the secret of all time. *5/3/95*

Freedom in the soul gathers freedom in the earth. Freedom in the heart gathers freedom in the soul. It is a time of measuring out, assimilation, gathering. A time of being helped into understanding. You are to one another One, reflecting identicalness. Look not into the other as the other one, but as the Self of you reflecting back that which is I AM. The power of light exposes all darkness, to bring forth the Light. Light only remains when the illusion of the darkness disintegrates as a shadow in the light of the Son. *6/1/95*

*W*e are not complete without each other. We are whole in each other complete. Our love is a circle of eternal life. The Vesica Piscis is the pinnacle in union to which now rests. Herein we are One. It is herein we are One. And that outside of that circle in the two circles is our individual expression of the one in form, split in time only. At the center of this Vesica Piscis we find ourselves unionized. Here we are the light Twin Flame burning!

Focus now on this idea. Corresponding units of Light, forever entered into the realm of service, project energy of same like energy. Law of Correspondence here below I AM you are. Fortress of eternal life gathers more energy as more light gathers the fortress I AM. The projection to which you now aspire requires information from collected I AM. That which you aspire to be cannot be accomplished in separate I AM identity. Information comes collectively, DiadrAna One. Measure of light to one equal One. Another entwined forever in the Tree of Life. There is no separateness in all. Once begotten, once beget, once allowing, once beget, once giving, once beget, once I AM you are I AM. *6/8/95*

*R*eunion - meaning what is important in our hearts for living in a finite world being infinite. Offer it up to reunion, meaning I AM you, you are me, we are I AM. The Word made flesh. The Word is infinite, to the flesh it is finite, and we need to bring it together in One. And when we do, we shall merge totally, allowing the cellular structure of the finite form to know its infinite possibilities. We are together in union, and we are together in union, and we are to gather in union ... many!

We spin in time - together. And when we are spinning in love, that's what unites us. When I fall out of love, I fall out of the spin. And when you fall out of love, you fall out of the spin. If one of us falls out of the spin of love, we separate. Now, in order to stay in ... the spin, we must stay in ... love. And the more in love we stay, the faster we spin. And the faster we spin, then we are allowed to ascend. Much like energy. It transcends the faster it spins. *7/15/95*

We are the two in One, the I AM one two.
You in me and I in you.
I support you.
More correctly, I embrace you.

To the fullness of that expression
to which you have yearned, I shall be
forever supportive of Thee.

I help you and you help me.
And when you help me, you help you,
And when I help you, you help me.
And each time we do this, we help the other one.
Until all are gathered,
remembered in the Only Begotten Son.

So we are a multitude,
one among many,
many among One.
We are all the Only Begotten Son,
forever.

And now we return remembering.
We return remembering.
Complete.
7/29/95

The holy light of God rests among all people. In the beginning was this holy light encountered in each other One. Too many worlds to be remembered as One. Children of love sitting upon the throne of God, awakening in dimensional worlds for co-creative potential. Love begetting its own energy gives forth its own light, according to that design within the idea.

There is no stopping this light frequency, for it's a natural frequency moving with time, increasing in its own Self, I AM.

Beget only love among each of you now. Foreign matter scatters. Allow the Light to absorb that to which it has been scattered as a Pac Man does in the tinker toys of your search for God. Loving life is about joy, joy, joy. Keep on with the energy to which you now find yourself in joy. It is delight.

Love is about giving one another an extended heart, opening the doors within the soul with a welcome energy field of I love you.

Be with I AM Myself in you as often as the moment can contain itself within your hold of memory into time. Gather into your lightwave a permanent understanding of the present moment frequency of the power of I love you. This practice can be encountered with the one whom you love. Think on that which you love the most. Allow the energy to fill you as much as possible in any moment of memory. This energy shall go forth in its own time, as allowing shall be that to which you are, and in the frame of reference to which you find your physical form, it shall consume it. Thus, that to which you live in the body form shall be that to which you are in the heart, each one unto the other one I love you frequency of I AM. And thus, we have a new beginning in the idea of DiadrAna, the flame of love made flesh remembered in the Light Being able to mirror its own Self in the flesh. This is true co-creation as we are about. The awaking of this will allow you then to understand new worlds to which you shall be sent in co-creation. Do you grasp this idea? *9/8/95*

The Thirsty shall thirst again
no matter what
nor where nor when.

I AM eternal life in Christ, and so are you.
And we are living waters
forever pouring through.
Seek ye this--I love you.

Ye shall be eternal and true
forever in I AM.
Thus you shall live forever in one land
again, again, again
forever more returned
unto that to which you are sent
to give unto yourself
the living waters of I AM.

So be it in time and in out of time.
So be it in space and in out of space. So be it in all I AM.
So be it I AM you are all I AM.
So be it I AM you are I AM Om Aum.
9/16/95

It is the will of our Father to be known in one union returning to the marriage of mystical union in the one heart of the I AM. It is so with all of those upon the earth at this time, cumulating in the accumulating of I AM. Love is One. Love is One. And so we are entering into a circle, if you will, of light among the many and the few, gathering strength and multitudes. So it is with the love of Jesus as he calls forth that which is His own. I AM you are I AM. *11/21/95*

Seek ye with wisdom what ye seek in time.
Let go of all thoughts except Mine.
Allow My energy to fill your space.
I AM full of holy Grace.
Beckoning now the call of love.
Seek to be this Presence in all.
For it is true you are that I AM.

Wisdom teaches speak not much.
Allow the energy of Christ.
Give it space and voice in all there is to know.
It will teach you all.
I promise you so.

Keep with loving one another.
It is all the measure that you need.
Let not your hands do what your heart would not hold.
Trust each person in your life.
Treasure it as gold.

Seek ye first the Kingdom of God.
Give unto others that which you have given unto you.
Rest in the assurance you are the Light of Christ.
Trouble not your hearts, for they trouble others.
Be not a house divided. Let one house stand among you.
The love of Christ is about I AM. So be it with you all.
Holy Light of God I AM you are.
You are my temple in which I shine My own idea.
My light is present in all.
Energy is present in all, and thus My will carries it.
I believe in that which is given to be known. So be it with you.
Resist not knowledge which it is given you to know.
Sleep in peace forever in units of two.
Synchronize your eternal watches of time to One.
Open, open, resist not.
Walk in the Light.
The measure of love is I love you. So be it with you and you and you.
You are my river of life. Rest in your own.
Love one another as I AM loving you now, and have and always shall.
I AM there. You are here. We are One.
Let not your hearts be troubled, for they trouble others.
Trouble not, never, never, never.
Speak words of peace in silence.
Caress the idea of loving One, One, One.
Hold I love you. *12/12/95*

*W*e are one another's love in each other's eyes to which we see capacities for loving greater depths. Let us now be free to give and love one another so that we can be free to give and love one another again.

We are the same. Twin Flame, twin light, holy energy of light, compassionate idea and voice of God, corresponding measures, holding patterns of I love you, corrective measures of precious moments.

Ascension

*A*scension.
It is a matter of growing old ... in love.
Compared to eternal life
it is the measure.
And so be it with ascension minds
and heart's readiness to empower.
Believing there is only this hour.
No other time shall be in this.
For time itself is not.
Eternity is all there is.
Ah, the mind!

Look beyond the tower to which your eye can see
or the fartherest speck to which you can grasp in Me.
This Ascension is the way to which the ladder climbs.
Out beyond the space to which the eye can see and the mind.
Ascension is allowing that which is beyond all knowingness
to draw you near its rim.
Then being willing to be "pushed,"
or take a step within your own.
So be it with Ascension.
No mind can grasp the wisdom herein given to *this* time.
For it means a place far beyond the mind.
You are one with God,
and God alone can see Ascension,
for He placed the ladder for you to climb.

Allow each foot to be moved by the drawings forth from above.
Pushed yes, from below, but drawn from above.
So be it with you. How else could you climb?
Could you possibly fall aside now,
placed in the middle of the forces,
pushed from below and drawn from above?
Oh no. Allow my energy now to do this in you.
And thus it is to Ascend. *12/30/95*

[This message was received from the I AM presence of the Master Jesus regarding his ascension with his Twin Soul, Mary Magdalene.]

I beheld her (Mary) later from a vortex of energy not in the present earth. It was important that I, the masculine energy form, go first, and hold for her, allowing her to spiral spin. Because of that which was given by Me, a separation, a sacrifice, leaving her in the belief that she was that which I AM known, allowed this energy form to take precedence in the earth so that two by two can beget ... not one two, not one two separated. You shall now enter into that vortex as a one two begotten one. Not necessary to do singular motion in transmutation of the I AM beloved one in the Twin Flame. THAT is the great sacrifice given ... that and that alone. It is now time for the Only Begotten to arise together as One. As I held the light for my beloved Mary, the light which she was holding for me drew unto itself I AM. Thus, we are united in eternal life One two, One two. *5/25/95*

Now, let us center our light in the Christ
which abides in all.
And resting here we find ourselves,
for we are One, you see.
And identification with the One
which we know to be,
brings forth the galaxy
of I AM in you and you in Me.

Master Teachers, oh I AM. Yes, I AM.
So be it with you now.
Seek ye not this own idea for yourself?
Where else could it be gotten from
but that which is in you to become
remembered in the Spirit of the Lord?

And as the energy of ideas comes together in love, each one of you now, calling forth a greater expression of your true Self, gathers information according to the love vibration. This love vibration is a unit of One. The information for you to be given now at this time is a peacefulness in the heart that is required for the union to take place in all. 1/4/96

Embraced now by the energy of eternal Om,

the one and only begotten Son of God comes home.
Through you, children of the Light,
to which I have found My own,
I give of Myself I AM.
Love one another in the eternal light to which ye stand
Press not against the walls of time,
but allow them to crumble on their own.
Seek ye the wisdom of the ages from on high,
for herein it is given you to know. *1/30/96*

Spirit Speaks
On
Twin Souls

On the evening of October 19, 1996 we had an unusual experience in that the Spirit of DiadrAna invited us to ask questions. John (Ana) responded to this invitation with questions directly related to the subject of Twin Souls. We offer this as a separate segment in this section since it seemed to synthesize all the fragments of Twin Soul information we had received over the past two years. "A" is the abbreviation for Ana who is asking the questions. "D" is the abbreviation for Diadra, through whom the answers were presented.

CA: **Speak to us of the origin of Twin Souls.**

D.: The Jesus Christ light of love in the beginning I AM. And the Master taught of the Twin Soul Light within the heart of each child gathering unto Himself those in love. Mastership is about that idea coming now. The Holy Light of God began in this way, saith I AM to all. The light descended in the time warps to which you understand of Being. We shall not understand how it came to be, but *that* it came to be. And as we await the Master's touch to this idea shall we hold the Light I AM.

CA: **What are Twin Souls?**

D.: I love you, DiadrAna. This is the Word made flesh, the idea that you seek. In the beginning the Light is about a lowering of Itself to manifest. Keep this idea simple as it is explained in the earth. The Word is the Light of God. This word is the Light of God I AM. To become I AM in I AM we must idealize that which is given, so we are about moving in times to be that which is I love you. The world to which you await now begins again a new idea. In the world we are one Light among the many and the few. This idea is akin to that which you know to be companions in hearts - one idea loving one idea, saith I AM. The world knows not the idea yet to be understood by many, but this is a beginning, so to speak, of this understanding.

In the beginning the Light lowered Itself to polarize in the majority of worlds to which akin this one began life forms. As each of you split into that form, being the opposite sex of the other one, the worlds became known through a consciousness vibration able to attest to itself through experience. The mastership of the vibrational frequency to each Light contributed to the mastership of the vibrational frequency of the other. Thus, the idea of twinsoulship was born. And the Master said unto the multitudes, "do you know one another? No, you do not! But I shall teach you through love." Coming into earth, the begotten daughters and sons of God multiplied, bringing forth that to which allowed that which is to be I AM. So over a period of times, the multitudes came to know the Self as love. And so be it with each in One. I love you, DiadrAna, saith I AM in you now. Be ye at peace. The center point from which Thou hast been One all along now resists not that which is to come.

That which is the Love Force at the center of that One to which now belongs the other One is about returning to the remembered state of union. And each Light frequency empowers the other one by loving. It makes no difference that to which finds Self, but which is about the loving context to which all Lights return. Say ye with the heart of One, "that to which is love shall be." And in that remembering I AM. "I believe that which is coming to pass," saith the I AM in you, allowing this state to be the reference point to which I love you moves forward in time. That light frequency begins to spin at a higher vibrational idea, and as the idea makes itself known in the one to which it spins, the love quickens in the other.

So much to be remembered in the union, so much energy to be released. Allowing penetrating through the vortexes of the mind, then the heart can be the opening, the central point to which I remember. Let us now begin this work into which we shall spiral forward, for a union in the earth is a magnificent occasion for two beings to experience, for to experience that of the flesh is the ultimate of the trine I AM. The multiplicity of complexity involved here is the mastery to which ye came to become.

Polarizations of energies are necessary for manifestation to be viewed and to be experienced at a level of itself that before in Spirit form is not possible. Allowing that energy to surface at times is a great undertaking of involvement. Be sure that you are ready for this, for it will require the ultimate sacrifice of the heart which holds on to any good thing. You must know that as you release, then that opens the door to embrace the greater good always. And mastership in union of the Twin is required to release all attachments. Nothing can be held. Nothing can be held. All must be allowed. This is not a light teaching, so consider it carefully as you move forward in this work. Do not become attached to the message. Do not become attached to each other, for in the realized state of being there is no attachment. There is only I AM. If you shall abide in the Twin Soul love in the earth, then that to which is given you must be understood.

You are about the love of Jesus Christ as that of before.
Having mastered the heart will give you an open door.
Leave us now not in temptation, saith the Lord God within,
but move forward I AM I AM.
Take no thought about the where, the when,
the how, and the why.
Let the mind be at rest. I AM I.

Seek with the heart to be remembered. This is important. Let the desire rise in you. Seek I AM. In this way, that which is sought is always found. That which is given is to be known. Written herein. Twin Souls are the beginning of I AM to which returns unto Itself a galactic unit of inblissness. Therefore, we are One. Yesterday is that which has brought you here. Today is that which carries you forward. Now allowing the times within that to which you seek to know. Be of good cheer. It shall be given. Multitudes are now coming to this point to which the love within them draws unto themselves I AM. Thus, Twin Souls return. I AM.

Q.: **How do Twin Souls reunite?**

D.: They unite through the power of that which is love, understood from a center beyond that which you now rest. It is a place in the heart, so to speak, that is the experience of the Divine I AM. It is sought within the individual idea of Light manifested as male or female. Herein this Light fully realized attracts the counterpart of the other One. It is much like a mountain stream so flowing from within itself not knowing from whence it came nor where it goeth, but allows that force to draw it back to Source. Return in the stillness to that which is the fragrance of love. Seek it always above everything that seems to matter. Let not the mind rest above the heart, for this keeps that which is the opening in the I AM shut. Allow the door in the heart to be opened by the impulse to know I AM love. It is a simple memory. It is not easy to carry forth in the world which the mind defines itself in attachment.

A.: **What else can we specifically do to allow for the reunion?**

D.: Nothing. There is nothing that can be done, except desire to love. This is the impulse from our God, and if we follow that impulse, that which seems to be a task in the earth to be done shall be given unto you. You shall know on a momentary basis that which love requires. Keep it central in the heart. Desire to love and love alone. Nothing else is a matter here. Nothing else is a matter here. Love Me now as I love you. Simple.

A.: **Are Twin Souls uniting now more than before?**

D.: Only to the degree that love returns to itself. Such is the beginning of I AM I AM.

A.: **What is the purpose for Twin Souls reuniting?**

D.: Measures beyond this one are to be opened in times. Nothing shall be revealed until that which is revealed is *known.* When the knowing of one idea becomes the resting and the home within the heart, the impulse of the divine destiny within opens another I AM yearning. And thus, that which is to be given shall be. You do not get this idea, for now you are contained. Yet, in the union of the two, it shall be known I

AM. And as I AM is gathered in I AM, you shall know again that to which you seek is that which is seeking to be made known manifesting in beyonds.

A.· **What is the difference between the relationship of Twin Souls and the relationship with other souls?**

D.· The difference is ideas. Each is an idea in God mind, so to speak, of itself in a full expression of Light. That which is formed in the beginning as a Twin Soul goes forth from the heart of God, much as a child does from your I AM presence in the earth, creating and experiencing life as I AM allowing God to be God. Each idea of Light is a soulmate of sorts to which ye are one in light frequency. The Twin is the Divine Counterpart in resonance with the other. Ideal, identity, identical, frequencies match. It is a pair of One; a unit of One; a collage of One in all form in mass, Spirit, body, soul, realms above, higher octaves; all one energy mass Lord in Light. Mastership requires I AM to be allowed its perfection.

A.· **Why is there conflict between Twin Souls?**

D.· The journey of each individual soul is designed and yet, at the same time, it is allowed. That which comes together as that which is the state of knowing determines the conflict in the mind of each individual. If there is less than love remembered in all states, this creates the conflict, for nothing can conflict with love. And love is what I AM you are. To remember this, all must be transformed to that degree of idea. So, when the Twins come in union in I AM, the mirror is the mind, each mind showing the other one what it seems to know, to the degrees of alignment of the heart's flame. Thus, we have either I AM harmony or I AM confusion. Return confusion knowing simply that it is a non-reality form established in the home of the mind. Take no thought to that which creates the conflict other than to know that if that entity feels conflicting, it is not of the Divine Love. The mind then with its great gift of freewill needs to take that which it seems to know and bring it to the Light within. This is all that is needed. *Resolve is intention to become the Light.* That is the way it is with love. *Resolve is the intention to become the Light.*

Q.: **What brings about the remembrance of union?**

D.: Just what I said, my darling. L-o-v-e. You cannot determine HOW this shall be done. Ye can only experience ye are I AM One. That which is I AM One is I AM One. To know this is to *be* in love. As this intensifies in knowing to you now, the time shall come when that which is known in each shall come to such a vibrational idea of itself, that it slips into a new spaciousness of mind and heart. It simply becomes a matter of knowing. I AM you are already One. That which seems to be apart is that which keeps in your heart the idea that we are not. So when the idea is released, a new idea is replaced. Rested in for a number of light particles to which find resonance in time fields, opens the door to knowing. Love is that frequency which stills time. For here we have I AM. Know this stillness as the One. It is already - not to become.

A.: **Why are some Twins not both reincarnated at the same time?**

D: Each finds an avenue through which the Light can express. The matter of, shall we say "programmed realities," is a matter of consciousness given unto each one at the time of I AM. The process through which learning is acquired comes from the impulse of the Divine Self. Experiences in many worlds are necessary for that which I AM is to remember its purpose and meaning. Impulsed by choice from on high, that which is seeming individual chooses in alignments and moves forward to experience that Divine Plan. Multitudes of ideas are gathered along in each dimensional experience of life, until such time as that design for which is in the seed of each soul reaches a maturity of expression to remember I AM. In this idea, we allow the Christ to become Itself to gather unto that which is to be a creator in I AM. Going forth now merged with Self in fullness, It creates the worlds to which the Divine Idea seeds again. The plan is intricate. The multitudes are many. And that design to which you find yourself is the idea impulsed in only you. Many children of Light will soon understand that each idea of Light created in the idea of Light has within it written that which carries forth the tapestry of eternal life, complementing every other eternal life idea. Thus, we have a glorified heaven. Nothing is the same, and yet we all are One.

A. **How can we best release the states of remembrance that are not in love?**

D. The power of God, this is the way. Keep with your ideas allowing each one I AM. Seek with all your heart to give unto the other one the love you feel for yourself. Be not afraid to hold each idea which is in opposition to your own. Continue with the word I AM. Help is given to those who ask. The purity of your heart will decrease that which ye seek not to remember.

Jesus is our guide. The world is I AM. Your hearts are being purified, DiadrAna. So much has been accumulated to what is not true. Only love is. The presence of the Almighty, that which is I AM, seeks only to reveal Itself. Simple. The heart is open if you will I AM be. There is only love. Once that idea begins to accept itself, the world can become a glorifying place for God, and YOU are set free. When that which you call "energy" comes up, it is a state of I love you, but it has been clouded by the mind that puts a page over a page. Quickly see this as it is and step back in rest. Close your eyes and become still - a moment of intended heart's will toward I love you. This is the way. Our Master we are. The love of God we are. Eternal life we are. Peace I AM. If you would, live in I love you. Then be that idea. For some reason, Children of Light make the choice not to be that idea, and yet they say they desire it with all their hearts. Confusing. What can disturb a light? Nothing. The light shines on everything revealing its beauty, or what you call unbeauty, never judging one idea, never placing one idea as more important than another. It just shines on. It allows all ideas to be. It sees all in the same light, and it gives of itself the same energy to all. Be as the Light.

So many times your mind says, "I want peace." That which is within you speaks against the idea. Bring that within you to the Light. Let it become still and see itself in the Light that is given unto it. It shall disappear and be absorbed into the Truth the Light reveals. I love you.

Q.: **Can Twin Souls incarnate into male or female bodies that are not of their own polarity?**

A.: The world is not ready to understand this great Truth. A Light becomes polarized, reduced in frequency to enter into the earth's atmospheric idea. Each time this occurs, it is the soul which determines the body form. The soul is the Light of God remembered or unremembered. To the degree that it is of the Light, it shall choose according to that design. To the degree that it is not of the Light, it may confuse its idea and choose that which is not of the synchronicity of the vibrational field of the polarized energy. That which is given to be remembered often times, however, can be remembered by the error choice. So be it all one I AM.

Q.: **What is the purpose for the reunion of Twin Souls?**

D.: To glorify God. Simple. To make known unto itself the complete whole idea of Light as a full extension of the Light. What is the purpose of having children in the earth? It is the same - to give life unto life. Returned, remembered gathers strength to begin new races of ideas. Such is the return of the two in the One - to give birth to new races of ideas, complete and whole, creating only image and likeness of the Light which knows itself I AM.

A.: What is the most important message about Twin Souls?

D.: Carry forth in your heart that idea of yourself. This attracts to you your own. Herein abides the I AM. The other Self that ye seek is I AM you are. Only here will you find that one to which your heart yearns. And ye will know in time I AM there, drawing unto you each one the Self to which ye yearn. I believe. Seek it with your heart. I AM.

A truth that can be received in the mind
will assist the hearts to open, to find.
The world needs My Light in you
and the understanding of One - not two.

That which gives the world the Light
is the beginning of the end of night.
That which is in the DiadrAna seed
holds the world itself, indeed.

And questions from the hearts of Light
to come and recognize I AM.
Return I love you.
So mastership, above all else to love abides.

DiadrAna, you are that which I AM resides.
Allowing Myself to teach and stretch
beyond your boundaries of the mind
gives Me an opportunity
to be a Light for others to find.

I have sent Myself in you,
a twinsoulship of One - not two.
For gathered in my name I AM
masculine, feminine
together again.

Myself reunited in the One
the whole becomes complete.
And in the earth this mastership

is a symbol of that to which is final
to this dimension of experience.

And those who recognize this
as the joining of the One
shall come to me again
One by One by One.

Each attracting that to which
the center from them is
I love you
in oppositeness finds its home.

The One returns remembered
carrying with it the bouquet of the
eternal life,
the sweetness of the knowledge of all
the love that creates again
from that which is the heart of God.
And there can be no error states
from this state in the One
that comes through life in earth
returned.

Many shall follow in this way.
Ye may not see it today,
but in the days to come.
The earth moving from I AM Om
to Aum
beckons those to which can accept

the Truth that we are all kept
in the heart of God, the one Light.

The earth returns a spiral spin.
Jesus Christ is held within.
Seeking hearts shall find again
I AM.

And that to which the soul is
I AM returned
shall be revealed its equal.
That which is the other Self returned
 I AM.

Union is that which is Divine
experienced by all
in a dimension of time, somewhere.
Each shall find a home,
and gathering the knowledge gained shall go again,
opening that to which the God within shall reveal.   *10/19/96*

In the beginning,
Eve was taken out of Adam.
In the end, the rib returns. 7/27/94

Recommended Book & Tape List

Twin Souls - (A Guide to Finding Your True Spiritual Partner), by Patricia Joudry and Maurie Pressman, M.D., Carol Southern Books (1995 ed.)
> Can be ordered through:
> New Leaf Distributing Co.
> 401 Thornton Rd.
> Lithia Springs, Ga. 30057
> Phone: (770) 944-2313 or
> Crown Publishing 1-800-793-2665

Embracing the Beloved - (Relationship As a Path of Awakening), by Stephen and Ondrea Levine, Doubleday (1995)
> Can be ordered through:
> DeVorss & Company
> P.O.Box 550
> Marina del Rey, Ca. 90294-0550
> 1-800-843-5743
> California residents: 1-800- 331-4719

I Remember Union - (The Story of Mary Magdalena),
by Flo Aeveia Magdalena, All Worlds Publishing (1992)
> Lesley Waldron
> 145 Flanders Rd.
> Bethlehem, Connecticut 06751
> (203) 266-5060 - Fax: (203) 266-7614

Ramtha Intensive: Soulmates, Channelled through J.Z. Knight, Sovereignty Inc. (1987)
> P.O. Box 1277
> Rainier, Wa. 98576
> Contact - Belinda Dawson
> (360) 446-6644
> Fax: (360) 496-6882

Also available, **Ramtha Video, "Soulmates"** from Sovereignty Press

Twin Souls and Soulmates - **St. Germain**, Channelled through Azena Ramanda and Claire Heartsong, Triad Publishers USA, Inc. (1995)
23623 N. Scottsdale Rd., #D-3 (146)
Scottsdale, AZ 85255
Ph: (602) 585-4287
Fax: (602) 585-2871

Soulmates, by Jess Stearn, Bantam Books (1984)
Can be ordered through:
DeVorss & Company

The Ascended Masters: On Soul Mates and Twin Flames (Book 2, Vol. 28), by Elizabeth Clare Prophet, Summit University Press (1988 ed.)
Box A - Livingston, MT 59047-1390
(406) 222-8300

Love and Awakening: Discovering the Sacred Path of Intimate Relationships, by John Wellwood, HarperPerennial (1996)
10 East 53rd Street
New York, NY 10022

John of the Cross - **(Selected Writings) (The Classics of Western Spirituality),** edited by Kieran Kavanaugh, O.C.D., Paulist Press (1987)
997 Macarthur Boulevard
Mahwah, New Jersey 07430

Nine Faces of Christ - **(Quest of the True Initiate),** by Eugene E. Whitworth, Great Western University Press (1980)
Can be ordered through:
DeVorss & Company

The Search for the Beloved - **(Journeys in Mythology and Sacred Psychology),** by Jean Houston, Jeremy P. Tarcher, Inc. (1987)
Can be ordered through:
DeVorss & Company

Predestined Love: You Were Born Again to be Together,
by Dick Sutphen, Valley of the Sun Publishing (1996)
<u>Can be ordered through:</u>
DeVorss & Company

The First Love Stories - (from Isis and Osiris to Tristan and Iseult), by
Diane Wolkstein, HarperPerennial (1991)
10 East 53rd Street
New York, N.Y. 10022

The Mystic Quest - "An Introduction to Jewish Mysticism",
by David S. Ariel, Schocken Books (1988)
Random House, Inc.

Decoding Destiny - Keys to Mankind's Spiritual Evolution,
by Tanis Helliwell, T.A. Helliwell Publications (Canada 1988)
212 Woodfield Road
Toronto, Canada M4L 2W7
(519) 853-1808 or (416) 469-8010

The Way of Passion - "A Celebration of Rumi", by Andrew Harvey, Frog,
Ltd. (1994)
<u>Distributed by:</u>
North Atlantic Books
P.O. Box 12327
Berkeley, Ca. 94701

Wheels of a Soul - "Kabbalah Reincarnation", by Rabbi Philip S. Berg,
Research Centre of Kabbalah (1991)
200 Park Ave., Suite 303 E
New York, New York 10166

The Shared Heart, by Barry Vissell M.D. and Joyce Vissell R.N., M.S.,
Ramira Publishing (1984)
P.O. Box 1707
Aptos, Ca. 95001
1-800-766-0629

To Love And Be Loved- (**The difficult yoga of relationships**) (audio-taped workshop), with Stephen & Ondrea Levine, Sounds True (1996)
> PO Box 8010
> Boulder, CO 80306
> 1-800-333-9185

Walking Between the Worlds, by Gregg Braden, Radio Bookstore Press (1997)
> P.O. Box 3010
> Bellevue, Washington 98009-3010
> 1-800-243-1438

Twin Soul Reunion: A Mystical Journey of Love (2 Tape Video Set) with John & Diadra Price, Wings of Spirit Foundation (1996)
> 6757 Arapaho
> Suite 711, Box 345
> Dallas, Tx. 75248
> Ph & Fax (972) 233-2992

If you are interested in sponsoring a workshop in your area on Soular Reunion, call John or Diadra Price. You can contact them through the Wings of Spirit address or phone.

Wings of Spirit Foundation
6757 Arapaho, Suite 711, Box 345
Dallas, Tx. 75248

(972) 233-2992

Wings of Spirit
Spiritual Support Products Catalogue

The Return of the Dove
by Diadra
Item # 0001   Softbound Book **$12.95**
Item # T001   Audio Book on Tape
(3 tape set) **$15.95**

This word for word message, received from the Holy Spirit, gives information, guidance and messages that quicken the remembered consciousness of union. Spirit speaks to us about:

> ~The Tree of Life
> ~The power of Omni Ashni
> ~Prestance, the Elixir of Love
> ~Messages Written in *Your* Heart
> ~Beyond the Reasoning Mind
> ~Empowerment to Ascension

Holy Spirit Regeneration
by Diadra
Item # T002   Audio Tapes (4 tape set) **$19.95**

This live recording of Diadra's workshop explores the depth of the purification process and the individual soul's journey in the Divine Plan. Among the topics addressed are:

> ~Regeneration of Soul & Body
> ~The Soul's Awakening Journey
> ~Mystical Prayer Techniques
> ~Baptism with the Fire of Spirit
> ~The Collective Initiation

Grace Awakening
by Diadra
Item # T003   Audio Tapes (2 tape set) **$13.95**

Taped live from one of Diadra's courses held at Unity Village, Mo. New concepts are presented on this little understood subject. An inspired teaching which moves consciousness from karma to grace as the soul awakens to its divine inheritance.

Twin Soul Reunion Video
John & Diadra Price with Patricia Joudry
Item # V001 (2 VHS Video Tapes)   **$39.95**

Embark on a mystical journey of discovery into a profound spiritual subject -- the missing link in the grand adventure of the evolution of the human soul. Explore the concept of the Twin Soul as an expression of the Light of God lowered in frequency to enter manifestation as masculine and feminine polarity for the purpose of awakening the full potential of co-creatorship in divine love. John and Diadra interview the co-author of the book *Twin Souls: A Guide to Finding Your True Spiritual Partner.*
Topics covered include:

~The Birth of Souls
~Who & What is a Twin Soul
~Twin Souls/Soulmates
~Shared Realities
~Polarity & Complimentarity
~Process of Reunion

Soular Reunion: Re-Membering of Self, Soulmates & Twin Souls
by John and Diadra Price
Item # 0002   Softbound Book   **$12.95**

This manual of love is an all inclusive study of the evolution of the human soul from the original split of the One masculine/feminine being into the masculine or feminine being you now find yourself to be. It integrates the principles and laws of consciousness governing the return to love and union with Self, soulmates and, ultimately, with your complimentary masculine or feminine Self. It takes an in-depth look at the Seven Sacred Mirrors of all relationships as well as addressing specific questions about Twin Souls and soulmates. The manual concludes with a word for word section from the Spirit of DiadrAna on the subject.

Wings of Spirit Order Form
(972) 233-2992

Item No.	Qty.	Description	Price	Amount

Subtotal

Shipping and Handling

(Payment must be in U.S. funds only)   **Total** $_____

Shipping rates as follows within USA only:

Price	UPS	Mail
Up to $15.00	$4.50	$3.25
$15.01 - $50.00	$5.75	$4.75
$50.01 - $80.00	$6.75	$5.75
$80.01 - $99.00	$8.00	$6.75

Allow 5 - 8 days for UPS and 3 - 4 weeks for 4th class mail - Prices are subject to change.

Mail orders to: Wings of Spirit Foundation
6757 Arapaho Rd. - Suite 711 - Box 345
Dallas, Tx. 75248

Ship to: (Please use street address if UPS delivery is selected)

Name:_____

Address:_____

City:_____State:_____ Zip:_____